D0008469

Voyages into Michigan's Past

Voyages into Michigan's Past

By Larry B. Massie

Avery Color Studios
Marquette, Michigan
1988

Library of Congress Card No. 88-70890
ISBN-0-932212-58-1
First Edition - April 1988
Reprint - 1989, 1989, 1990, 1991, 1992, 1994

Cover artwork reproduced from
original artwork by Frederic Remington, 1908

Cover by Diane Tedora

Published
by
Avery Color Studios
Marquette, Michigan 49855

Dedication

For Wallace Bruce Massie, my father, who taught me to love history.

TABLE OF CONTENTS

Foreword

It was a happy choice when Booth newspapers contracted to publish Larry Massie's weekly features on Michigan history to help commemorate our state's sesquicentennial. The series proved popular with newspaper audiences across the state, and so it is especially good that Avery Color Studios has made it available in more permanent and accessible form. Michigan has been a much "underwritten" state - a shame, because it has enjoyed a rich and exciting past and has made numerous and important contributions to our nation's growth. This collection from Massie's pen will help to educate, entertain and enlighten the present, and it is hoped, future generations of Michiganians. Larry Massie has a sure eye for the interesting and significant in Michigan's development and is obviously at ease whether writing of *coureurs de bois* or auto industry magnates.

All too often readers have been turned away from the vital and exciting story of Michigan's development by dull, unimaginative, and let's face it, pedantic writing styles. Massie's collection does not suffer from any of these flaws, and on the contrary, maintains a blend of sprightly style with accuracy of historical detail that should please a wide audience. The causes of Michigan history and of so-called popular history are enhanced by this excellent collection. In short, this book, whether read at a continuous sitting or savored by means of spot reading, constitutes a most enjoyable and worthy addition to the literature of Michigan history.

Some years ago it was my good fortune to have Larry Massie enroll in several of my classes while he was working toward his degrees from Western Michigan University. He not only loved and collected books—he mastered what they held between their covers, and to no one's surprise, he graduated with high honors and became a professional writer and historian. Thus, it is with much pride and pleasure that this collection of Larry's work is recommended to all who enjoy history and good writing.

Alan S. Brown
Western Michigan University

Preface

It's a remarkable place, this great mitten of land surmounted by a rugged upper peninsula. More fresh water laps its shores than at any other place on earth. It's the Wolverine State, the land of Hiawatha and the arsenal of democracy all rolled into one. It has been home to the celery city, the cereal city, the furniture city and Motown. It gave the world the Republican Party, the tin lizzie and the hairiest baseball team in history. Voyageurs and Indian chiefs, shanty boys and Cornish copper miners, the man with the branded hand and the man with the window in his stomach, the king of Beaver Island and the king of harem heaven once strutted its stage.

In this volume, I have tried to capture some of the glitter of an historical development that, for color and romance, takes a back seat to no other state. This is a book for Michiganders, native-born, adoptive or unfortunate enough to be living elsewhere. I hope I have provided you with a means to savor the nostalgia of half-forgotten times, to explore our heritage and celebrate our accomplishments.

The 52 essays in this collection originally appeared during Michigan's sesquicentennial observance in the Kalamazoo Gazette, Grand Rapids Press, Muskegon Chronicle, Jackson Citizen-Patriot, Ann Arbor News, Saginaw News and Bay City Times. I have restored information that was deleted in some newspapers because of space limitations. I have also included a bibliography of my sources that will guide those interested in further reading.

My sincere gratitude goes to the Booth editors who made the series possible. Jim Mosby, editor of the Kalamazoo Gazette, and Mary Kramer, metro editor of the Kalamazoo Gazette were particularly supportive throughout the project. Dave Person of the Kalamazoo Gazette proved an expert copy editor who spared me from committing several historical faux pas. My wife Priscilla maintained her usual sweet disposition, as she devoted many hours to the hot lights of the photographic copy stand. Al Beet of Allegan performed masterful photographic processing.

My special thanks go to the newspaper readers who encouraged me to make the series available in a more permanent form.

Larry B. Massie
Allegan Forest

The Fort with an "Indifferent Palisade"

Eau Claire artist Jan Frazer's conception of Fort St. Joseph.

The log palisades of Fort St. Joseph and the bark-covered buildings huddled around them loomed dark against the snow at the first light of day. All was still; a blanket of ice muffled even the nearby St. Joseph River.

Suddenly an Indian dog barked out a warning. Then came the crunch of running feet and the clank of weapons as a force of Spanish and French soldiers and Indian allies rushed the gate. It was all over in a matter of minutes, the fort captured and the sleeping garrison taken prisoner without a shot being fired.

The resident Potawatomi joined the attacking band of Milwaukee Indians in looting the fort and outbuildings as Captain Eugene Pouré mustered his troops before the post flagpole. The British ensign was yanked down and replaced by the royal Spanish colors. Pouré stretched open a proclamation and read: "I annex and incorporate with the domains of his Very Catholic Majesty, the King of Spain, my master, from now on and forever, this post of St. Joseph and its dependencies with the river of the same name, and that of Illinois, which flows into the Mississippi River."

It was February 12, 1781, the one and only day in Michigan history when a Spanish flag waved triumphantly over a portion of its territory. The French and British standards had preceded and the stars and stripes would follow in the 19th century. In honor of this brief event, Niles, the present downtown of which lies roughly one mile north of the site of Fort St. Joseph, calls itself, "The City of Four Flags."

The French had established Fort St. Joseph on the west bank of the river in 1691. Count Louis de Buade Frontenac, governor of New France, sought by its presence to prevent the local Indians from trading with the British. In 1694 the small garrison withstood an attack by several hundred marauding Iroquois. Until the founding of Detroit in 1701, Fort St. Joseph was second in importance only to Michilimackinac, and it remained the major military post in western Michigan.

Nevertheless, visitors depicted the fort as being in a dilapidated condition. Pierre Charlevoix, who sojourned there in 1721, wrote: "The commandant's house, which is a very sorry one, is called the fort, from its being surrounded with an indifferent palisado." Sometime after Charlevoix's visit, the fort was moved to the east bank of the river.

French and English rivalry over the fur trade erupted into a final conflict in 1754. The French surrendered Fort St. Joseph to the British in 1759 but did not evacuate it until two years later. Thomas Hutchins, a British engineer who inspected the fort in 1762, thought it "to have been intended more as a place for traders to put their effects in than a work of defense to keep the natives at their proper distance."

Hutchins' theory was tested the following year when a band of seventeen Potawatomi inspired by Chief Pontiac easily seized the fort and killed or captured the British garrison. The Indians held the fort for over a year. Illinois historian Edward C. Mason wrote in 1886: "Fort St. Joseph had been so uniformly taken and plundered whenever anyone set out to do it, that capture had become its normal state, and seemingly the object of its existence." Fort St. Joseph's unfortunate record continued into the Revolutionary War.

During the early years of the war, Col. Henry Hamilton of Detroit, the dreaded "hair buyer," armed Indians and sent them on forays against the American frontier. Col. George Rogers Clark carried the war to the west in 1778 when he led a force of Virginia militia into the Illinois country. He occupied the Mississippi river posts of Cahokia and Kaskaskia and won over the allegiance of the local Indians.

Spain, to whom France had ceded the territory west of the Mississippi in 1762, declared war on Great Britain on June 21, 1779. The following year a large British and Indian force from Michilimackinac traveled down the Mississippi to attack Cahokia, Kaskaskia and Spanish-held St. Louis. The Americans and Spanish learned of the campaign, made a mutual-aid pact and repulsed the British and Indians.

A French officer, Augustin de la Balme, led a company of volunteers from the Illinois country on a campaign to capture Detroit in October 1781. In concert, a detachment of 16 men from Cahokia under command of Jean Baptiste Hamelin moved against Fort St. Joseph. They attacked while the Potawatomi warriors of the village were on a hunt and easily overwhelmed the fort. Hamelin's men took 22 prisoners and a valuable cache of trade goods and supplies and retreated towards Chicago. However, Lt. Dageau de Quindre, in command of a British force stationed nearby to protect the post, quickly raised an Indian war party and set out in pursuit. They overtook the raiders near the Calumet River, killed or captured all but three, and recovered the booty.

When news of this defeat reached the Mississippi River posts, El Heturno and Naguiguen, chiefs of the Milwaukee Indian band, convinced the Spanish commandant at St. Louis, Don Francisco Cruzat, to launch a retaliatory strike against Fort St. Joseph. On January 21, 1781 Cruzat sent out a force of 65 Spanish and French soldiers and sixty Indians under command of Pouré, his militia captain.

Pouré's men ascended the Mississippi and Illinois Rivers until they reached a point where the latter was frozen over. Whereupon they disembarked and made a twenty-day march fraught with "all that can be imagined of cold, peril and hunger." On February 11, the Spaniards camped for the night a few miles from Fort St. Joseph while interpreter Louis Chevalier, son of a St. Joseph fur trader then being held captive at Michilimackinac, went ahead and convinced the resident Potawatomi to remain neutral in exchange for half the booty to be taken in the raid.

Pouré's force crossed the frozen St. Joseph River at 7:00 the next morning and captured the sleeping fort. De Quindre's contingent was apparently absent at the time. After plundering the post and flying the Spanish flag for a few hours, Pouré burned the fort and retreated with his spoils and prisoners. De Quindre was unable to convince the Indians to pursue. Pouré arrived back at St. Louis on March 6 and presented the captured British flag to Cruzat.

The Spanish raid proved relatively unimportant in a strategic sense, but it provided Spain with a claim to the territory east of the Mississippi which it pursued without success during the treaty negotiations in Paris in 1782. Fort St. Joseph was never rebuilt.

The Imprisoned Priest

The Rev. Gabriel Richard, the first priest to serve in the U.S. Congress.

Father Gabriel Richard raised the little silver spoon heaped with snuff to his nose, squeezed one nostril shut and sniffed deeply. The violent sneeze that reverberated through the cell block in the Wayne County jail nearly sent his spectacles flying. The priest gazed out through the barred window in the four-foot-thick wall and considered his plight. Fellow French novelist Alexandre Dumas could not have invented a more fantastic plot.

It was October 10, 1824, and Richard, Michigan's duly elected territorial representative to Congress, had been incarcerated without bail for failure to pay a court judgement on a libel suit. Not only was Detroit's St. Anne's Church bereft of its priest, but with Congress about to reconvene, his presence was required in Washington.

Far from a criminal, Richard was one of Michigan territory's most illustrious residents. Born in Saintes, western France on October 15, 1767, Richard received a classical education at the local college and then entered the seminary at Angers conducted by the Sulpician order. He was ordained a Sulpician priest in 1791, amid the French Revolution and anti-clerical movement. The young priest immigrated to Baltimore, Maryland the following year. Finding the ecclesiastical seminary there oversupplied with priests, he took charge of a remote Illinois mission.

In 1798 Richard transferred to Detroit, which had been evacuated by the British but two years before. Most Detroit inhabitants were of French ancestry but, as English was the dominant vernacular, he began to study that language. In addition to his normal parish duties, Richard soon embarked on an ambitious campaign to improve Detroit's educational and cultural condition.

He established a school for boys in 1804 and soon lent his support to a young ladies' academy staffed by four women he had trained. Much of his early effort was spent rebuilding the dilapidated old St. Anne's Church. When he finally had it in serviceable condition, it and practically every other building in Detroit were leveled by fire in 1805.

During a trip east in 1808, Richard acquired and shipped back to Detroit Michigan's first piano and organ. He also purchased a printing press and several fonts of type. The press, a supply of paper and journeyman printer, James Miller, arrived in Detroit during the summer of 1809. John McCall had operated a press in Detroit during the 1790s, but since 1800 the city had been without a printer.

By August 1, 1809 Richard's press had produced *The Child's Spelling Book,* the first book to be printed in Michigan. The first and only issue of Detroit's pioneer newspaper followed on August 31. The four-page *Michigan Essay; or Impartial Observer* contained nothing in the way of local news, but citizens did learn for the first time of world events that had occurred some two months before. From 1809 until the press ceased operation in 1816, James Miller and succeeding printers turned out over 50 Detroit imprints, including books of law, religious instruction and poetry in English and French.

Much of Richard's energy was spent in fund raising to build a new St. Anne's Church. By 1818 he had secured enough capital to lay the cornerstone. But he soon ran out of funds and resorted to various moneymaking enterprises, including a commercial fishing operation. He also followed the example of local businessmen by paying his workmen in scrip. Unfortunately, a local printer forged several hundred dollars worth of 50-cent "shinplasters" in Richard's name and flooded the countryside with them. Mortified, Richard nonetheless ultimately redeemed the bogus scrip with his own funds. In 1828 a grand new St. Anne's stood complete.

In the meantime, Richard had ventured into diverse undertakings, including support of a mission at Mackinac Island, a professorship in the first University of Michigan established in 1817 and politics. Friends who thought the French element was being neglected approached him to run for the office of territorial delegate to Congress in 1823. He accepted in order to further his plans for more educational facilities and Indian missions. The $8.00 per day salary earned by delegates would also benefit St. Anne's building fund.

During his campaign he realized he had never applied for U.S. citizenship as required by law. But the Wayne County Court granted him citizenship. In a bitterly fought election Richard narrowly defeated John Biddle, a member of a prominent Philadelphia family, and Wayne County Sheriff Austin Wing. Biddle contested the election based on the one year citizenship requirement. A congressional committee eventually ruled in Richard's favor. He became the first priest to sit in Congress.

Richard's old-fashioned breeches and silk stockings, peculiar French accent and incessant snuff taking became the talk of Washington that winter. When Congress adjourned during the spring of 1824, Richard returned to Detroit to find that his newly-made political enemies had been busy brewing trouble.

It seems that following usual church procedures Richard had excommunicated Francoise Labadie in 1816 for divorcing his wife and remarrying via the civil court. Richard also reprimanded Labadie sharply, calling him a "scandalous sinner." As a result many parishioners shunned Labadie, and he lost his job.

Labadie sued Richard for libel and in 1821 won a judgement of $1,116. The priest appealed, but despite the concurring opinions of such legal giants as Henry Clay and Daniel Webster, upon his return to Michigan in 1824 the local court confirmed the original verdict. An hour later Sheriff Wing escorted Richard to the Wayne County jailhouse.

Richard languished in jail for three weeks before bond was approved and posted. Under its provisions, he was not allowed to leave Wayne County. He cited congressional immunity, however, and left for Washington in late fall. During that session Richard performed notable services for the territory, including persuading the government to build the first road across the peninsula, the Detroit to Chicago Military Road (present day U.S. 12).

Richard lost a bid for reelection in 1825 by four votes. He was never again permitted to leave Wayne County. When a cholera epidemic broke out in Detroit in 1832, Father Richard nursed the sick and dying until he succumbed to the disease. His body lies beneath the nave of the present St. Anne's Church.

He Trampled the Union Jack

Lewis Cass, territorial governor of Michigan.

The flotilla of cargo canoes rounded a bend in the Saint Marys River and headed for the shore at the frontier settlement of Sault Ste. Marie. The stars and stripes flapped from the stern of the lead canoe carrying Michigan Territorial Governor Lewis Cass. As they strained against the strong current, the oars and paddles of the voyagers glistened in the setting sun. Half-breed children playing at the water's edge darted for cover when they spied the gleaming bayonets of the blue-coated soldiers on board, but a throng of Indians fired a salute of welcome and cried "bosho, bosho," the traditional north country greeting.

The expedition headed by Cass had left Detroit on May 24, 1820. It numbered 42 men including Henry Schoolcraft; James Duane Doty, who would become territorial governor of Wisconsin in 1841 and of Utah in 1863; eleven infantrymen; and various other scientists, voyagers, Indian guides and hunters. An additional 22 troops had joined the party at Mackinac Island. It was June 15 when the squadron of canoes reached Sault Ste. Marie. The men immediately pitched camp on an open field near the river.

Secretary of War John C. Calhoun had authorized the expedition to gather scientific data and to assert American authority in the Lake Superior and upper Mississippi regions. The native Ojibwa had sided with the British during the War of 1812 and war parties from the Sault had sacked and plundered the Michigan frontier. Cass, who had distinguished himself as a military commander during the war, had also become an inveterate Anglophobe. He suspected further British intrigues to incite the northern tribes against the Americans. His immediate objective at the Sault was to secure a treaty to allow the establishment of a fort at that strategically important gateway to Lake Superior.

The roar of the rapids and the dull throb of tom-toms

from the Indian village located on a ridge some two hundred yards to the west allowed the Americans little sleep their first night at the Sault. The following morning, Cass established rapport with the matriarch of the Sault, Susan Johnston, daughter of a powerful Ojibwa chief and wife of Irish fur trader, John Johnston, then away on a visit to Ireland. As the troops erected a large marquee, Cass summoned the chiefs to parley.

The chiefs arrived in their finest ceremonial costumes. British medals dangled from the necks of some. The Indians squatted under the marquee while Cass distributed tobacco, gaudy trinkets and other presents, and soon the peace pipe passed around the circle. Then Cass, through an interpreter, announced his mission. Long ago the Indians' ancestors had ceded occupancy rights to the French and those rights had now passed to the United States, he stated. A murmur of disagreement arose as the chiefs, eyes flashing, spoke among themselves.

One group seemed inclined to accept the American claims provided there was no garrison established at the Sault. Understanding their point, Cass quickly replied: "As to the establishment of a garrison they need not give themselves any uneasiness — it was a settled point, and so sure as the sun that was then rising would set, so sure would there be an American garrison sent to that point, whether they renewed the grant or not." This decisive statement brought more animated argument among the Indians. Head chief Shingabawassin, tall, stately and wearing a feathered headdress, spoke for moderation. Shingwauk, or the little Pine, who had led the last war party from the village in 1814, sided with the hostile faction.

Then Sassaba, known as The Count because he wore a scarlet British uniform jacket, with epaulets, stood up, hurled his war lance into the ground and began gesticulating wildly. He had lost a brother in the Battle of the Thames in 1813 and harbored a deep hatred of the Americans. His angry address brought the parley to a close. As the chiefs filed out, Sassaba contemptuously kicked away the pile of presents.

Returning to his encampment, Sassaba defiantly hoisted a British flag before his lodge. Cass instantly ordered his men on alert. Then, unarmed and with only his interpreter, Cass marched down the ravine and up the slope to the Indian camp. He yanked down the British flag, trampled it into the ground, entered Sassaba's tent and told him "the United States would crush him and his nation in the same way." Cass wheeled and calmly walked back to his own camp.

Had Cass approached the Indian camp with an armed party there would undoubtedly have been a battle. But he stunned them with his courage, a trait held in high esteem by the Ojibwa. Nevertheless, a few minutes later, when the women and children of the camp took refuge across the river, the Americans prepared for an attack.

But none came. The chiefs had sought council with Mrs. Johnston and she had convinced them of the futility of resisting the Americans. Later that afternoon at a second council the chiefs acknowledged American authority and ceded a 16 square mile tract at the Sault.

The next day Cass and party continued on their exploratory tour which would ultimately reach the Mississippi River, 4,000 miles in all. Two years later Colonel Hugh Brady arrived at the Sault to construct the fort that would carry his name.

Sassaba relinquished his British uniform for a wolf skin robe, but he continued to nurse his hatred of the Americans. On Christmas day 1822, while returning from a drunken spree at Point aux Pins, Canada, nine miles west of the Sault, his canoe capsized and he and his family were swept down the rapids and never seen again.

Intrepid Cass went on to greater glories. He continued as territorial governor of Michigan until 1831 when he became Andrew Jackson's Secretary of War. He served as Minister to France from 1836 to 1842 and represented Michigan in the U.S. Senate for twelve years beginning in 1845. Cass ran as Democratic candidate for president in 1848 but was defeated by Zachary Taylor. Wealthy and an influential elder statesman, Cass died at Detroit in 1866.

The Song of Manabozho

Henry Rowe Schoolcraft, famed Indian researcher.

The cold Lake Superior wind howled as it piled snowdrifts against the birch-bark lodge. Inside sat half a dozen Ojibwa braves, as many squaws, some with papooses, and one white man. The smoke from a flickering fire stung the eyes of those ranged around it. A squaw poked the fire, and it blazed up to cast eerie shadows on the lodge wall.

Then a wrinkled elder began to speak:

> A lynx, almost famished, met a hare one day in the woods, in the winter season, when food was very scarce. The hare, however, stood on a rock, and was safe from its enemy.
>
> "Wabose," said the lynx, in a very kind manner, "Come here, my little white one, I wish to talk to you."
>
> "Oh no," replied the hare, "I am afraid of you, and my mother told me never to go and talk to strangers."
>
> "You are very pretty," answered the lynx, "and a very obedient child to your parents, but you must know that I am a relative of yours. I wish to send some word to your lodge. Come down and see me."
>
> The hare was pleased to be called pretty, and when she heard it was a relative, she jumped down from the place where she stood, and was immediately torn in pieces by the lynx.

The old Indian settled back and another began his tale. He told of how Manabozho, messenger from the Great Spirit, was swallowed alive by the giant sturgeon, but returned to battle the king of serpents. And so it went around the circle, each brave relating another legend: of Mudjekewis and his nine brothers who conquered the Mamoth Bear and obtained the Sacred Belt of Wampum, of Puck Wuidj Ininee, the mischievous little wild man of the mountains and Mishosha, the magician of Lake Superior.

When the evening's entertainment was over, the white man, Henry Rowe Schoolcraft, returned to his house at Sault Ste. Marie and recorded these strange tales. He married a beautiful half-Indian maiden in 1823 and from her family and friends gathered many more traditional lodge tales. Others he collected as he traveled the Upper Peninsula in pursuit of his duties as Indian agent for the upper Great Lakes.

In 1825, Schoolcraft first published samples of oral literature of the Ojibwa in a book of travels. His two-volume *Algic Researches*, published in 1839, put many other examples in print. His compilation received scholarly reviews but little popular interest. One reader in particular, however, found Schoolcraft's Indian legends intriguing — Henry Wadsworth Longfellow. Using tales from *Algic Researches* and other Schoolcraft publications as a source, Longfellow fashioned an epic poem in a lilting trochaic meter borrowed from the Finnish national saga, *The Kalevala*.

Longfellow first titled his poem "Manabozho" but later shifted to Hiawatha, hero of the Iroquois version of the same legend. *The Song of Hiawatha*, published in 1855, became an immediate best seller and eventually took its place as one of America's most familiar examples of native folklore.

Schoolcraft, the pioneer ethnologist who had first recorded the Michigan Indian legends, was a man of many other talents. Born near Albany, New York in 1793, Schoolcraft developed an early enthusiasm for scholarship. As a teenager he published poetry and essays in local newspapers and edited his own manuscript magazine. He joined his father's glass manufacturing firm but was forced out of the business when the British saturated the market with cheap glassware following the War of 1812. Schoolcraft turned to the western frontier to seek his fortune.

His first book, published in 1819, was an account of the

Missouri lead mines. It won him a national reputation as a mineralogist and attracted the attention of Secretary of War, John C. Calhoun. Invited to Washington, Schoolcraft impressed president James Monroe and other cabinet members with his expertise. He was appointed geologist on an exploratory expedition to the upper Great Lakes. Headed by Michigan Territorial Governor Lewis Cass, the expedition left Detroit in May 1820. During the arduous four-month-long canoe journey across the length of Lake Superior to northern Minnesota, Schoolcraft cemented a firm friendship with Cass. Schoolcraft's account of his travels won him additional honors as a scientific explorer and author.

Although he could speak no Indian tongues, in 1822 Schoolcraft was designated Indian agent for the upper Great Lakes with headquarters at Sault Ste. Marie. At the Sault he was befriended by John Johnston, an Irish fur trader who had married the daughter of a powerful Ojibwa chief. A year later, Schoolcraft married Johnston's daughter Jane, known as the "northern Pocahontas." With the help of the Johnston family, Schoolcraft studied Ojibwa and began collecting lodge tales and other cultural data.

In 1832 during another expedition to uncharted areas of the Lake Superior Country, Schoolcraft discovered the source of the Mississippi River at Lake Itasca. The following year he transferred his agency headquarters to Mackinac Island. Appointed Superintendent for Indian Affairs for Michigan in 1836, Schoolcraft moved to Detroit but continued to summer at Mackinac Island.

Schoolcraft also served in the Territorial Legislature from 1828-1832, and helped found the State Historical Society in 1828. He supplied the name for fifteen new Michigan counties, many of which, such as Allegan, he compounded from Indian words. Schoolcraft resigned his Michigan position in 1841 but continued to travel over much of the American frontier collecting information on Indians.

In 1847 Schoolcraft went to Washington D.C. to serve as special agent in the Office of Indian Affairs. He spent the next decade compiling an monumental six-volume work on the history of the Indian tribes. It remains a primary source for the study of American ethnology.

During the final years of his life Schoolcraft suffered from crippling arthritis. His heart was broken when his two sons took up arms on opposite sides during the Civil War. Michigan's pioneer ethnologist, explorer and writer died on December 10, 1864 and was buried in the Congressional Cemetery in Washington. The village of Schoolcraft, located south of Kalamazoo, and Schoolcraft County in the Upper Peninsula honor his name.

Mackinac Island, Hub of the Fur Trade

Mackinac Island as drawn from Round Island, ca. 1820.

The big birch-bark canoe skimmed across the Straits of Mackinac heading for the humpbacked island the Ojibwas called "The Great Turtle." Nearly two tons of beaver, mink, marten and other valuable pelts had been crammed into the 30-foot-long craft. The crew, 10 French Canadian voyageurs, had stopped at nearby Pointe La Barbe to shave and don their finest apparel in preparation for the merriment they knew awaited them at Mackinac Island.

It had been nearly a year since they had seen civilization - long months of arduous canoeing and portaging, of trapping and trading with the bands of Indians they encountered. Now, with the white bulwarks of Fort Mackinac in view, 10 red cedar paddles dipped at a rate of fifty strokes a minute in rhythm with a traditional voyageur's boat song.

"Par derrier chez mon pere,
Vole, mon coeur, vole-"

The high prow of the craft cut through the waves, showering the men with spray, as the canoe sped toward the wigwam-lined shore. Within a few feet of crashing full speed onto the beach, the voyageurs simultaneously backpaddled with all their strength and the heavy canoe jerked to a stop. Fellow fur traders paused from their revelry to welcome the new arrivals with shouts of greeting and hearty back thumps.

It was the summer of 1822, the heyday of the Michigan fur trade. Long before Michigan's timber, mineral resources and farm lands were successively exploited, fur dominated its economy. Mackinac Island was the hub of a fur trading empire that stretched throughout the Great Lakes to the Mississippi River.

In the 17th century the French had recognized the strategic importance of the Straits of Mackinac, a bottleneck through which most upper Great Lakes traffic flowed. They ruled the fur trade first from Fort

Michilimackinac at present day St. Ignace. In 1701 Antoine de la Mothe Cadillac moved the garrison to Detroit, but within a few decades Fort Michilimackinac had been reestablished on the south shore of the straits at present day Mackinaw City.

The French continued to control the fur trade until their defeat by the British during the French and Indian War (1754-63). In 1781 the British constructed Fort Mackinaw on the more defensible heights of Mackinac Island. The Treaty of Paris in 1783, which ended the Revolutionary War, awarded Mackinac Island to the Americans, but the British refused to evacuate the fort until 1796.

At the outbreak of the War of 1812, a British contingent promptly forced the surrender of the fort before the American garrison even learned of the declaration of war. An American campaign to recapture the island in 1814 failed, but when hostilities ceased in 1815 the British again withdrew.

One result of the War of 1812 was the establishment of American dominance in the fur trade. Congress passed legislation that barred any but American citizens from trading on U.S. soil. Eastern fur, shipping and real estate magnate John Jacob Astor acted quickly to take advantage of the situation. In 1817 he located the headquarters of his American Fur Company on Mackinac Island.

Through adroit political maneuvering Astor gained special privileges that allowed him to run rivals out of business and gain a virtual monopoly of the fur trade. Territorial Governor Lewis Cass, for example, routinely granted Astor exemptions that permitted him to utilize skilled French Canadian voyageurs. The American Fur Company eventually employed 2,000 to 3,000 voyageurs and some 400 clerks on Mackinac Island. During the peak year of 1822, pelts valued at $3 million cleared Astor's post.

Each fall an army of voyageurs fanned out from the island to establish winter camps on isolated streams throughout the Great Lakes country. Great birch-bark cargo canoes conveyed up to four tons of trade goods such as guns, hatchets, blankets, gaudy trinkets and barrels of whiskey. In violation of federal laws against the trading of ardent spirits, nearly 9,000 gallons of whiskey were shipped to Mackinac Island in 1832 alone. Traders further stretched their liquor supply by watering it down and adding tobacco for an extra kick. Firewater, for which tribesmen might swap their entire winter's catch, was a recognized evil of the fur trade.

Despite the sizable profits realized by Astor and some of his subordinates, little in the way of financial rewards was passed on to the hard-working voyageurs. Boatmen received an annual salary of $83.00, out of which they supplied their own clothes and tobacco. Nevertheless, voyageurs were a colorful lot who chose their profession because they loved the freedom and adventure of the wilderness. They were capable of almost superhuman endurance.

Col. Thomas McKenney, who made an exploratory tour of the upper Great Lakes in 1826, marveled when his voyageurs paddled from 3:00 a.m. until 9:30 p.m. one day, a total of 79 miles. Numerous portages to avoid rapids or shortcuts across peninsulas required lugging the canoes and eighty to ninety pound bales of furs and trade goods over miles of rough terrain and swamps.

Each hour voyageurs paused briefly to smoke their clay pipes. Distances, in fact, were reckoned by the number of "pipes" it took to travel them. The only food consumed on journeys of several months duration was "lyed corn" (a type of hominey) and salt pork. Sometimes when pork ran out a ration of tallow sufficed.

The romantic era of the fur trader had become largely a thing of the past by 1840. Astor sold the American Fur Company in 1834, and the center of the industry shifted westward to St. Louis. The demand for beaver pelts also diminished when fashion favored silk over beaver hats. Mackinac Island's economy turned from fur trading to fishing. By the 1870s, the "fairly island" had become a tourist mecca. The fudge came later.

The Man With the Window in His Stomach

Dr. William Beaumont, medical pioneer.

The seething mass of Indians and French voyageurs that blanketed the beach of Mackinac Island, pitching tents, brawling and carousing, had just returned from a long season spent trapping and trading in the wilderness. It was June 6, 1822, the heyday of the Great Lakes fur trade, when Mackinac Island was the rendezvous for the entire north country. Eager to purchase moccasins, gaudy neckbands and other supplies, an unruly throng jostled one another roughly as they crowded into the American Fur Company store located at the foot of Fort Mackinac.

Suddenly a shotgun accidentally discharged. Alexis St. Martin, a 19-year-old French voyageur, fell to the floor, with a hole blown in his upper abdomen large enough to insert a fist. The full charge had entered his body, shot, wadding and pieces of his clothing. The muzzle flash, not three feet away, set his shirt on fire. Everyone thought him dead.

Someone ran for Dr. William Beaumont, the post surgeon, and he arrived within minutes. He found St. Martin still alive, but after examining the wound he expected the patient to die within twenty minutes. Nevertheless he cleaned and dressed the wound.

St. Martin, with a constitution hardened by voyageur life, fought to live. An hour later, Beaumont moved his patient to a more convenient place and began removing the shot and other extraneous matter from the wound. The damaged portion of the stomach adhered to the wound rather than falling back into the abdomen. This fortunate circumstance allowed the doctor to successfully treat the wound. Miraculously St. Martin survived. Within three weeks he had a hearty appetite and, except for the wound, was in perfect health. Beaumont tried to close the aperture in the stomach, but could not. St. Martin would live, but with a permanent hole in his stomach.

Unable to work because of the accident, St. Martin became a pauper. Mackinac County authorities callously refused him any assistance and made plans to send him back to his home in Montreal. In his condition, the 2,000 mile canoe trip would likely have proved fatal. But out of the kindness of his heart Beaumont took St. Martin into his own home, a very generous deed considering that he recently had married and subsisted on a salary of $40 per month.

Born on November 21, 1785 in Lebanon, Connecticut, Beaumont left home when 21 and settled at Champlain, New York, where he taught school for three years. In 1810 he began to study medicine under a physician in St. Albans, Vermont. He received his license two years later and immediately enlisted in the U.S. Army as a surgeon's mate. He saw active duty during the War of 1812 at Little York, Fort George and Plattsburg. When the war ended in 1814, Beaumont resigned and set up a private practice in Plattsburg, New York. Before long, however, he reentered the army and was assigned post surgeon at Fort Mackinac under command of Gen. Alexander Macomb, with whom he had served during the war. He arrived at his new post in June 1820.

St. Martin lived with Beaumont for nearly three years following his accident and had recovered enough to be able to chop wood and perform other chores. Sometime during that period, Beaumont conceived the idea of conducting experiments on his ward's digestive system. The hole in the stomach permitted observations of the organ in action. Heretofore, no appreciable progress had been made in the study of the human stomach. Beaumont's work, made possible by St. Martin's bizarre accident, would be a pioneering effort.

In 1825 Beaumont began introducing various types of foods, vegetables, meat, alcoholic beverages, etc., through the aperture in St. Martin's stomach. He studied the digestive process and took careful notes on how the stomach reacted to different stimuli.

Although these experiments caused him no pain, and he owed his life to Beaumont, St. Martin did not appreciate the proceedings. Not only was he superstitious, but the "man with the window in his stomach" suffered from the tauntings of his fellow voyageurs. Beaumont was transferred to Fort Niagara in the spring of 1825. St. Martin accompanied him, but soon took advantage of his proximity to Canada to desert his benefactor. For several years Beaumont sought in vain to discover his whereabouts.

Beaumont bounced around to several frontier posts. In 1827, while stationed at Green Bay, he located his wandering experimental subject. Not until 1829, however, could he convince St. Martin to join him at his new post at Prairie du Chien to continue his digestive investigations. St. Martin finally agreed to the distasteful line of work only after Beaumont offered him a salary higher than he could earn as a voyageur. In October 1832, Beaumont drew up a legal contract with his subject which stipulated that for monetary compensation he allow the doctor to feed him and observe his stomach. But when Beaumont permitted St. Martin a short leave home, he was never able to get him to return.

In 1833 Beaumont published a treatise on his observations, *Experiments and Observations on the Gastric Juice and the Physiology of the Stomach.* His work shed new light on the nature of gastric secretions and the process of digestion. It took the scientific community by storm and to this day remains one of the classic American contributions to medical literature.

Despite his achievement, the U.S. Congress rejected Beaumont's petition for a grant of $1,323.75 as compensation for his expenses in treating St. Martin. He resigned his commission in 1839 and established a lucrative private practice in St. Louis. Prior to his death in 1853, the "leader and pioneer of experimental physiology in America" received many honors from the scientific community.

Alexis St. Martin settled down in St. Thomas, Quebec, where he married and fathered twenty children. The "man with the window in his stomach" died at the age of 77 in 1880.

Hung by the Neck Until Dead

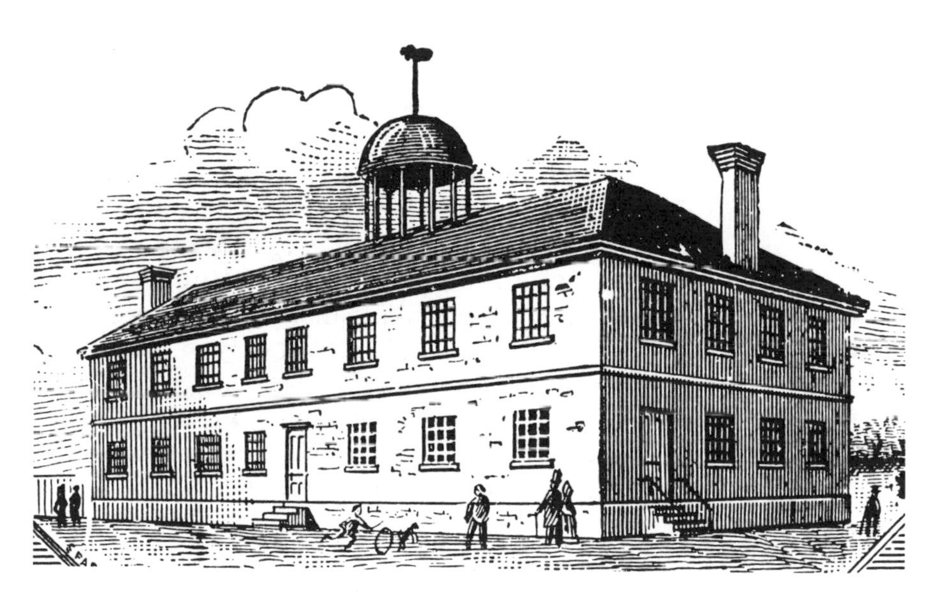

The Wayne County Jail erected in 1819, scene of the Simmons hanging.

The wooden grandstand creaked as the spectators leaned to get a better view of the condemned man. Fashionably-dressed ladies tilted parasols against the sun's rays. Frontiersmen sat atop horses at the edge of the crowd, and boys climbed nearby trees for the best vantage. Here and there a blanket-draped Indian stoically observed the proceedings.

Detroit's total population numbered barely 1,500, but an audience of 1,200 had assembled at the stone jail near the corner of Gratiot Avenue and Farmer Street on September 24, 1830. Some pioneers had ridden for days, and others carted along their entire families in buckboards. A military band, called out for the event, regaled the crowd with spirited martial tunes. Entertainment was mighty scarce in frontier Michigan, and settlers made the most of any spectacle.

Stephen G. Simmons solemnly strode to the scaffold flanked by the sheriff and a deputy. A huge man weighing 250 pounds, Simmons towered a head above his escorts. His normally ruddy complexion had turned ashen. But he mounted the ladder to the platform with a firm step and calmly faced the crowd as Sheriff Woodworth read the death warrant.

Demon rum lay at the root of Simmons' predicament. Pioneer Detroiter Edwin Jerome remembered Simmons as "a man of culture and education transformed from a debonair to a debauchee by that deadly enemy of man, ardent spirits." Simmons operated a hotel and tavern at Wayne, some thirteen miles west of Detroit on the road to Ypsilanti. A genial host fond of entertaining guests, Simmons tossed off many a toddy by way of hospitality. So many, in fact, that he became an alcoholic, and when drunk, his character changed from affable to angry. He took to arguing loudly with customers, and when in his cups beat his wife and two daughters.

One night in one of his uglier moods, he tried to force

his sick wife to drink with him. When she refused, he punched her in the stomach, a blow that killed her.

Arrested and brought to trial in Detroit, Simmons faced a tribunal of Judges William Woodbridge, Solomon Sibley and Henry Chipman. Local opinion was firmly antagonistic toward Simmons because of the nature of his crime and his reputation as a mean drunk. Over 300 jurors were sworn in before 12 could be found who had not already made up their minds.

Simmons' two daughters testified that when sober, he was a loving husband and father, but when drunk had "previously beat their mother a hundred times, each harder than on the fatal occasion." Defense Attorney George A. O'Keefe argued eloquently that "a drunken man was not responsible for his whims," but the jury found Simmons guilty of murder.

The Rev. Calvin Colton, a traveling author visiting Detroit, observed the court proceedings. He wrote that as the judges sentenced Simmons to death by hanging "he wept - he sobbed, his inmost soul heaved with anguish; he bore the marks of contrition."

Wayne County Sheriff Thomas S. Knapp refused to act as a public hangman. Whereupon Uncle Ben Woodworth, colorful Detroit pioneer and proprietor of the city's most famous early hostelry, the Steamboat Hotel, announced he would be glad to perform the duty. Territorial Governor Lewis Cass quickly appointed Woodworth acting sheriff.

Uncle Ben, whose Steamboat Hotel boasted the largest billboard in the city, had a well developed flair for showmanship. He supervised the construction of a quadrangular grandstand and mustered the Detroit City Guard Band for the occasion. Following his reading of the death warrant on September 24, Sheriff Woodworth carefully adjusted the noose, and asked Simmons if he had any final statements to make.

Showing no fear, Simmons addressed the crowd in a

resonant voice. He confessed his guilt, forgave everyone who had a part in his sentencing and said that if he "had his life to live all over again, would shun all spiritous and intoxicating liquors." He made a final plea for the mercy of the court and Governor Cass, and then sang a familiar hymn of the time in a rich baritone:

"Show pity, Lord, O Lord, forgive,
Let a repenting rebel live;
Are not thy mercies full and free?
May not a sinner trust in Thee?
My crimes are great, but can't surpass
The power and glory of Thy grace,
Great God, Thy nature hath no bound,
So let Thy pardoning love be found."

When he finished the hymn, "one loud, simultaneous, sympathic sound gushed forth from twelve hundred surrounding voices." Woodworth led Simmons to the trap door beneath the heavy beam that supported the rope, and pulled the lever. He died quickly of a broken neck.

Simmons' execution left a profound impression on the spectators. One young eyewitness later wrote that the experience led him to "think such punishment both cruel and vindictive." The Simmons hanging helped create a widespread public feeling against capital punishment. In 1846 Michigan became the first state to abolish capital punishment for murder.

"The Indians Are Upon Us!"

Chief Black Hawk, from the McKenney and Hall collection.

"The Indians are upon us!" shouted the galloping horseman. Startled from his sleep, Michigan militia Major Hosea Huston peered in amazement from the sole frame structure that stood at the site of what would become downtown Kalamazoo. E. Lakin Brown, territorial Michigan's version of Paul Revere, made his midnight ride in the spring of 1832.

Earlier in the evening, a messenger from White Pigeon had swept into Schoolcraft with news that the Indians in Illinois had gone on the warpath. Acting Governor Stephens T. Mason had called out the Michigan militia to go to the relief of Chicago. Brown, a Schoolcraft storekeeper, volunteered to alert the other settlers.

The following morning, most of the able-bodied men of the county rendezvoused at Schoolcraft. Armed with every conceivable type of firearm, including some of Revolutionary War vintage, the Kalamazoo troops made up in enthusiasm for what they lacked in military bearing. A few days later, orders arrived for the Kalamazoo regiment to march at once for Niles to link up with the main body of territorial militia.

The depredations of Black Hawk, a 65-year-old subchief of the Sauk tribe, had caused all the excitement. He had fought on the British side during the War of 1812, taken scalps at the River Raisin Massacre near Monroe and remained an inveterate enemy of the Americans. Not that he did not have good reason. In 1804, representatives of the Sauk and Fox nations had ceded some fifty million acres of land in present day Illinois, Wisconsin and Missouri for a paltry annual payment of $1,000. But the treaty also stipulated that the Indians should continue to "enjoy the privilege of living and hunting" upon the land.

About 1823, squatters moved in and took possession of rich lands at the mouth of the Rock River in Illinois that had long been cultivated by Black Hawk's band. Black Hawk's repeated appeals to the American government for protection went unheeded. Each year brought additional encroachments and indignities. Black Hawk resolved to fight for possession of his ancestral village.

Black Hawk withdrew to the west side of the Mississippi in 1831, but the following spring he led 1,000 of his followers back to the Illinois shore. On May 14th, a handful of his warriors routed an advance division of the Illinois militia, which the Indians had caught drunk in camp. The Sauks then conducted a series of bloody raids on northern Illinois settlements. Refugees retreated, and word of a mammoth Indian uprising spread like a prairie fire across Illinois, Indiana and Michigan. Michigan pioneers were certain Black Hawk would head for Detroit, pillaging and plundering along the way. With every telling the horrors grew worse. Settlers near Chicago huddled within the walls of Fort Dearborn. Illinois Governor John Reynolds appealed for help to President Andrew Jackson and the governors of nearby states and territories.

Twenty-year-old Acting Governor Stevens T. Mason responded immediately. He declared a state of emergency and mobilized the territorial militia. At the same time, General Hugh Brady set out for Chicago with two regiments of federal infantry stationed near Detroit.

Major General John R. Williams, commander of the Michigan militia, balked at following Mason's orders. He proclaimed that he would not move until ordered by Governor Porter, because Mason as acting governor had no ex officio power as commanding officer. But when Mason issued an official proclamation ordering Williams to raise volunteers and proceed to Jonesville to link up with a force from other outlying areas of the territory under command of General Joseph Brown and published it in the newspaper, the cantankerous old general gave in.

Williams assembled local militia regiments at Dearborn and marched along the dusty military road toward Jonesville. Along the way, volunteers from every hamlet and town joined the force. At Jonesville, five companies of volunteers from Palmyra, Clinton, Adrian, Blissfield and Tecumseh swelled the ranks of Williams' 8th Michigan Regiment. Williams rendezvoused with Brown's contingent at Jonesville and then rode back to Saline to muster in additional volunteers.

While at Saline he received a disappointing letter from Mason. Since a large detachment of regular army troops was enroute to Fort Dearborn, the Michigan militia was to be disbanded at once. Furious, Williams dashed off a letter to U.S. Secretary of War Lewis Cass, a former Michigan governor, complaining that, "The orders of the acting governor are inconsistent, contradictory, and incompatible with military rules."

General Williams decided to proceed to Chicago anyway. He caught up with the 8th Michigan at Niles. General Brown had already discharged them, and the dejected volunteers were heading home, minus the glory of battle. When E. Lakin Brown and the other militiamen from Kalamazoo County reached Niles, Brown also ordered them to return. Williams countermanded Brown's orders, but by that time most of the men were so demoralized by the flurry of contradictory orders that they ignored Williams and trudged home.

Nevertheless, Williams collected a small force, including remnants of the militia from western Michigan under command of Lieut. Col. Abraham Edwards of White Pigeon and a cavalry unit from Detroit, and pushed on to Fort Dearborn. He arrived on June 8th and took charge of the fort until the arrival of the U.S. army force. When a detachment of 300 cavalrymen from Indiana arrived, Williams ordered the Michigan troops home on June 22.

Meanwhile, General Winfield Scott was proceeding toward Chicago with various detachments of regular army soldiers from the East Coast. They embarked on steamers at Buffalo and arrived in Detroit on July 4th. Aboard ship on Lake Erie, the deadly Asiatic cholera broke out among the troops. Scores died at Fort Gratiot, hundreds more deserted in panic and the contagion spread to the civilian population of Detroit. When what was left of Scott's force reached Chicago on July 10, they were forced to convert the entire fort into a hospital.

By the end of July, the plague had been checked. Scott set out to deal with Black Hawk, but he was too late. A force of Illinois militia and regular army soldiers had annihilated the Indians at the Battle of Bad Axe on August 2nd. Of the 1,000 Sauks who crossed the Mississippi in April, 1832, not more than 150 survived the tragic Black Hawk War.

They Fought for Toledo but Settled for the U.P.

Governor Stevens T. Mason, who led the Michigan militia to the Ohio border.

Michigan Governor Stevens T. Mason led his territorial militia toward the Ohio border. Mason's rag tag army, 250 strong, jauntily stuck feathers in their hats as a mark of insignia. Those without firearms shouldered broomsticks.

Across the state line, Governor Robert Lucas, who had called for 10,000 volunteers to resist the invasion, mustered his own makeshift army.

It was 1835, and Michigan and Ohio were about to go to war over a plot of land known as the "Toledo Strip."

The seeds of civil strife had been sown in the Ordinance of 1787, in which Congress reserved the right to form one or two states north of a line drawn east and west from the southern tip of Lake Michigan. Unfortunately, the map used depicted the tip of Lake Michigan farther north than it actually is. The Ordinance Line appeared to intersect Lake Erie north of the mouth of the Maumee River, the present site of Toledo, Ohio.

In 1803 Ohio inserted a proviso in its first state constitution that provided for a redrawn boundary should the line actually prove to be south of the Maumee. In 1805, when Congress created the Michigan territory, it set as Michigan's southern boundary the Ordinance Line as drawn straight east from the actual tip of Lake Michigan.

Ohioans in Congress campaigned for acceptance of a more northern borderline. In 1817, U.S. Surveyor General Edward Tiffin, a former Ohio governor, employed William Harris to survey the line according to Ohio's constitution. When Michigan Territorial Governor Lewis Cass protested to President James Monroe, another survey was run by John A. Fulton in accordance with the Northwest Ordinance.

The area between the Harris and Fulton lines, the Toledo Strip, was eight miles wide at Lake Erie and five miles wide at the Indiana border, 468 square miles in all. Ohio continued to claim the tract, but the controversy died down as Michigan quietly assumed jurisdiction over the region.

Entrepreneurs platted the towns of Port Lawrence in 1817 and Vistula in 1832. The two were united as Toledo in 1833, a site investors thought destined to become the dominant city in the midwest. Eastern capitalists who wanted their Toledo investments under Ohio's jurisdiction lobbied Congress. The controversy entered the political arena in earnest on December 11, 1833, when Michigan sought admission as a state.

For over three years, Ohio congressmen blocked Michigan's bid for statehood. Only by accepting Ohio's version of the boundary could Michigan enter the union. "Never in the course of my life have I known a controversy of which all the right was so clear on one side and all the power so overwhelmingly on the other," former President and then Massachusetts Representative John Quincy Adams remarked during a three-hour speech in support of Michigan in 1836.

Meanwhile things were heating up at the border. When Territorial Governor George B. Porter died of cholera in June 1834, Territorial Secretary Stevens T. Mason became Acting Governor. Born of an aristocratic Virginia family, the 22-year-old Mason was fiesty, independent and determined.

When Governor Lucas rejected Michigan's offer to negotiate, the Territorial Council passed a resolution that imposed a stiff penalty on anyone other than Michigan or federal officers who attempted to exercise jurisdiction in the Toledo Strip. Lucas organized the disputed tract into a county named after himself and appointed a sheriff and judge. Michigan's "boy governor" mobilized the territorial militia, led his army into the no man's land, and the Toledo War was on.

Fortunately the Toledo War proved to be a relatively

bloodless affray. The only casualty was a Michigan sheriff stabbed during a tavern fight by a buckeye named Two Stickney. Mason's militia arrested some Ohio officials in the Toledo Strip, captured nine surveyors and fired a volley over the heads of the rest of the retreating survey party.

The war quickly became a comedy of errors. When the Ohio legislature voted a $300,000 military budget, Michigan voted $315,000. Lucas's judges held a hasty candlelit court session and retired to a nearby tavern to celebrate. After a round of drinks, the court ran into the night in panic when it thought the Michigan militia was approaching. In the excitement, the court clerk forgot his stovepipe hat containing all the official records.

President Andrew Jackson ended the Toledo War in September 1835 by removing Mason from office. General Joseph W. Brown, commander of the Michigan militia, immediately disbanded the troops. Michigan citizens set up a state government and elected Mason as governor. But Congress withheld official statehood until Michigan agreed to Ohio's claims.

On January 26, 1837, Michigan finally entered the union as the 26th state, minus the Toledo Strip. As compensation Michigan received title to the western three-quarters of the Upper Peninsula, 9,000 square miles of some of America's most valuable timber, iron and copper country. Not a bad trade!

Michigan's First "Cow College"

The two main buildings of the University of Michigan, ca. 1860.

University of Michigan freshman George W. Pray lay awake in his room on the fourth floor of Mason Hall thinking of how much he missed his home on the remote shores of Lake Superior. It was nearly 5 a.m. and he expected any minute to hear the hated clanging of the brass railroad bell that summoned the campus to arise.

Instead he heard expletives in an unmistakable Irish brogue. The bell was normally suspended from a third-story window of the hall. But some pranksters had shifted the apparatus to another window. University janitor Pat Kelly, whose duty it was to ring the morning alarm, could not find the bell's rope in the dark.

When he finally did find it, the bell pealed with considerably more than its usual intensity. Kelly then thumped up the narrow stairs to bellow into the rooms of every member of the student body, "Hey! Hey! Get up with ye! Didn't ye hear the bell?" That did not take him long because the entire enrollment of the U of M consisted of six freshmen and one sophmore.

It was the fall of 1841, the first term of the university that had been signed into law by Governor Stephens T. Mason on March 18, 1837. Presbyterian minister John T. Pierce and Isaac E. Crary, who became Michigan's first congressman in 1835, had drawn up a progressive school system that included a state-supported university.

Traditionally Congress allocated the proceeds from the sale of one out of every 36 sections in newly surveyed townships for the support of each new state's school system. Pierce and Crary's plan, which was enthusiastically supported by Governor Mason, provided for a portion of the "school sections" to be designated as "University lands" and be given to the state in perpetuity rather than to the townships, as was usually the case. Michigan's revolutionary plan slipped by unnoticed during Congressional approval, and the university received 48,000 acres of choice land by way of funding.

Ann Arbor won the site of the university chiefly because a local land company offered a free 40-acre tract. The first board of regents toured the pioneer settlement and by a margin of one vote approved acceptance of a flat field on the eastern outskirts of the village, then being farmed by a squatter named Pat Kelly. Kelly became the university's first janitor and, until he was discharged in 1847, his cattle, chickens and other livestock continued to roam over the campus of Michigan's first "cow college."

The regents appointed as the university's first professor Asa Gray, a promising young physician who would become one of America's most famous botanists. Since the university still existed only on paper, the board granted Gray a paid year's leave of absence and allocated him $5,000 to purchase a library for the university. He traveled to Europe where he secured an eclectic collection of 3,407 volumes in various languages from the noted publisher George P. Putnam. In 1840 freight wagons loaded with crates conveyed Gray's acquisitions from Detroit to Ann Arbor.

In the meantime, the university had suffered a series of setbacks. As a result of political intrigue, much of the valuable university land had been sold at discount prices to squatters and land sharks. The university's one million dollar endowment had shrunk by half. Upon his return from Europe, the regents were only too happy to grant Gray another leave of absence, this time without pay.

In the midst of a building campaign that featured four residences for professors, two large classrooms, a separate medical facility and a library building, the regents discovered they had barely enough money to pay for the residences and one classroom already under construction.

Governor William Woodbridge had succeeded Mason

in 1840, but he resigned the following year. His successor, John S. Barry, inspected the Ann Arbor site and announced, "Well, we've got the buildings.....I don't think they're good for anything else, so we might as well declare the University open."

As part of Crary and Pierce's original plan, a series of branch academies had been opened to prepare students for university work. Ultimately branches operated in Pontiac, Detroit, Monroe, Kalamazoo, Niles, Tecumseh and White Pigeon. Three branches closed in 1841, and the board appointed two of the unemployed principals as university professors. Reverend George Palmer Williams from Pontiac became professor of mathematics and science and the Reverend Joseph Whiting from Niles was named professor of Greek and Latin. Each received an annual salary of $500 and free house rent. In addition, the regents appointed Reverend Henry Colclazer as librarian at an annual salary of $100.

Colclazer and Williams were busy installing the university library in the third floor of the classroom which was later named Mason Hall when the first student, Lyman D. Norris from Ypsilanti, arrived to register. When classes began on September 25, six others had paid their $10 entrance fee. Students were also assessed $7.50 a year for use of the dormitory. They paid $1.50-$2.00 per week for meals, provided their own books and equipment, including candles, and were even assessed for any necessary repairs to university facilities. The average student paid $80 to $100 a year, a sum often equivalent to the entire cash income of their families.

The regents established a rigorous daily routine. Following Kelly's reveille at 5 a.m. came mandatory chapel at 5:30, breakfast at 6:30, the first class at 8:30, two hours for a noon break, study periods or classes from 2 to 5 p.m., followed by a vesper service. Students ate dinner at 6 p.m. and enjoyed free time until 9 p.m. when

Kelly rang the bell for lights out. They cut their own firewood, carried wash water up to their rooms and swept the floor and deposited ashes in the hallway. Kelly, who was soon dubbed "Professor of Dust and Ashes," collected the hall deposits.

Sundays featured mandatory attendance at one of Ann Arbor's churches. Despite sermons that might last as long as two hours, church provided one of the few occasions the collegians might meet village belles. Following a church service in 1844, George Pray recorded in his diary that "the girls possessed as many witching and enticing ways as usual - they hitched and twitched and showed their big bustles as much as ever."

Pray graduated at the university's first commencement exercise on August 6, 1845. He studied medicine at Western Reserve University and practiced in Ionia County until his death in 1890.

The Pioneers Got the "Shakes"

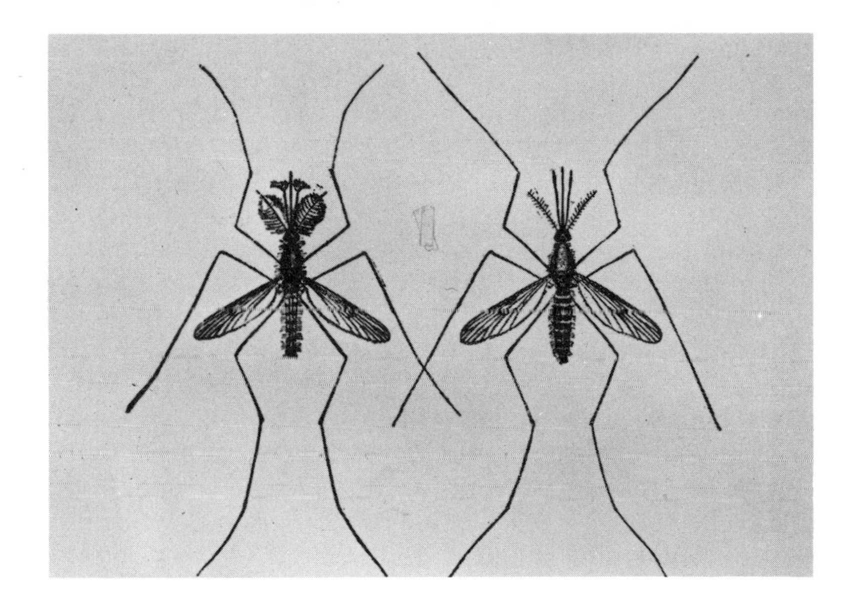

Anopheles mosquitoes, the villains behind the ague.

"Don't go, to Michigan, that land of ills;
The word means ague, fever and chills."

So ran a popular chant of the 1830s. The pioneers who fanned out across the southern parts of the peninsula in the 1820s and 1830s to carve homesteads out of the wilderness counted wild animals, loneliness, lack of creature comforts and backbreaking labor among the least of their worries. It was the ague (pronounced ā'-gue), what we have come to call malaria, that they feared the most.

Few, if any, escaped a bout with the disease. Lenawee County pioneer F.R. Stebbens remembered that during the fall of 1838 there were three persons sick with "chill fever" to every one well. Anson Van Buren, who settled in Calhoun County in the 1830s, described two brothers who were the last ones in the settlement to get the ague. They had begun to boast that they were immune to the disease when they both came down with an especially severe case. Martin Mapes, according to Van Buren, shook so hard that "the dishes rattled on the shelves against the log wall." Another account tells of workmen scrambling down from a roof they were shingling because the ague-ridden inhabitants shook the cabin so.

Frontier vernacular termed the disease the "Fev-Nag," the "Ag-in-Fev," the "Shakin Ager," or simply the "Shakes." Whatever they called it, pioneers quickly learned its symptoms. First came yawnings and stretchings and the fingernails turned bluish. Then, as Van Buren recalled, a cold sensation "crept over your system in streaks, faster and faster, and then colder and colder in successive undulations that coursed down your back." Following cold chills that set the patients's body to shaking came warm flashes that increased into burning fever. In a few hours, or sometimes several days later, the fever broke in a sweat.

Some patients experienced the cycle every day, others every other or third day, in a predictable pattern. The disease was so widespread that pioneers accepted it as part of life in Michigan territory and they learned to work around its disabling symptoms by dividing their calendars into "well days" and "ague days." Ministers, lawyers, judges and doctors scheduled their appointments so as to accommodate the "shakes." Housewives planned their washing, ironing and baking around times when they expected to be down with the "fits." According to Van Buren, beaus who "went sparking" on their well nights were sometimes disappointed to find their beloved chattering with the ague.

The ague made pioneer life miserable but rarely proved fatal. Yet many, weakened by its effects, succumbed to more virulent diseases. Doctors treated patients with diverse remedies according to their school of thought. Some victims got bled, or blistered by irritating poultices. Others swallowed massive doses of poisonous mercury compounds. The lucky ones received a prescription of "Peruvian Bark," the source of quinine and a genuine cure and preventative of malaria. By the 1840s refined quinine became available.

Those who could not afford a doctor or distrusted his hazardous techniques treated themselves with exotic folk remedies. Some recommended a dose of slippery-elm bark tea as an emetic. You had to be careful to shave the bark off with an upward stroke however; if you cut downward it would produce an opposite effect on the system. Others quaffed a brew of mullen and sassafras roots or swallowed three large pills made of cobwebs at the onset of the shakes. Van Buren tried what he had been informed was a sure cure. He pared his finger and toe nails, wrapped the clippings in tissue paper, placed the package in a hole bored in a maple tree and bunged up the hole. He distinctly remembered that his symptoms increased in severity following the experiment.

Pioneer physicians accounted for the disease with a number of imaginative theories. One school held that the ague came from the rotting vegetation produced by settlers cutting trees. Another that the disease was buried in the soil and released through plowing. The most common belief blamed the stagnant water standing in marshes from which emanated a "miasma," very unhealthy to breathe at night. Whatever the cause, pioneers early learned that the ague was more prevalent near swampy areas and avoided building nearby.

The answer seems obvious today, thanks to the work of Drs. Walter Reed and George W. Goethals who identified the bite of the mosquito as the true cause of malaria. But pioneers knew nothing of vector-host relationships. As late as the 1880s a researcher experimented to find that the use of window screens reduced the prevalence of malaria. But he theorized that the screens kept out minute particles of vegetation that caused the disease.

Commonly, when pioneers recalled their worst experiences they mentioned the ague and mosquitoes, sometimes in the same paragraph. But they never understood the cause and effect relationship. Mosquitoes were a nuisance that sometimes drove settlers off. Screens were unheard of. The sole protection lay in smudge fires, outside around the clearing during the day and within the cabin at night. The only way possible to milk cows at the height of the mosquito season was to build a smudge fire. The cattle learned to enter the protective smoke themselves. Pioneers considered eyes smarting from smoke far better than tormenting hordes of mosquitoes.

When settlers gradually reclaimed marshes for agricultural purposes and drained swamps to eliminate mosquitoes, the ague gradually disappeared in Michigan.

Commune on the Kalamazoo

A humorist from the 1840s satirized the Fourier Socialist experiments.

There has never been a decade quite like it. America's traditional urge for improvement blossomed during the 1840s into a national mania of reform. Theorists devised new remedies for mankind's sundry social, spiritual and digestive ills. Serious-minded reformers campaigned against slavery and for woman's suffrage. Others tried to improve their countrymen's lot via exotic diets, domiciles or dress. Still others sought salvation through a potpourri of imaginative new religions.

For some reason, an inordinate number of avante-garde movements emanated from western New York. Michigan, which drew a major proportion of its pioneer population from that region, also inherited a lion's share of eccentric beliefs. Transplanted to Michigan soil they flowered into unique contributions to American popular culture.

Based on a set of engraved plates he dug up near Palmyra, New York, Joseph Smith founded the Mormon church. After Smith's death in 1844, a splinter group of Mormons under "King" James Strang established a monarchy on Beaver Island. Modern American Spiritualism originated near Rochester, New York, in 1848 when three teen-aged sisters began communicating with the ghost of a murdered peddler. By the mid 1850s, numerous mediums, spirit rappers and ouija operators had made Battle Creek the midwestern headquarters for the sect.

William Miller, a New York state farmer, computed the exact date the world would end. When the time arrived in 1844, thousands of hysterical Millerites gathered on hilltops to await Judgment Day. Following their "great disappointment," a band of Millerites headed by James and Ellen White founded the Seventh Day Adventist Church. Sister White seasoned her dogma with graham cracker inventer Sylvester Graham's vegetarian precepts and a dash of hydropathy, which promised health through the healing benefits of water. By 1855, the Whites had moved their church headquarters to Battle Creek, where it operated a worldwide publishing empire. Later, when Spiritualist and Adventist ladies both donned the daring costume popularized by Amelia Bloomer, spiritual sparks flew in Battle Creek.

The antislavery movement germinated in Michigan to produce a prominent spur of the underground railroad. Traveling phrenologists, who critiqued character by feeling bumps on subjects' heads, found in Michigan a receptive clientele. Phrenologist publisher Orson Fowler invented the octagon house for healthier living, and soon the eight-sided structures dotted the Michigan countryside.

During the early 1840s, New York City editor Horace Greeley not only advised young men to go west but advocated a form of socialism. Devised by Charles Fourier, a mad French pholosopher, Fourier socialism advocated creation of phalanxes. All would live under the roof of one huge building, individuals would be employed according to their aptitude and profits would be divided 1/3 to capital, 1/4 to talent and 5/12 to labor. During the 1840s, at lease 25 Fourierist phalanxes were started in America. Most proved short-lived failures, but Brook Farm near Boston won fame as a result of participation by transcendentalist authors.

A young Ann Arbor physician responded to Greeley's advice and attempted the only Fourierist experiment in Michigan. Dr. Henry R. Schetterly, a small dark-haired man of German descent, arrived in Ann Arbor with his family of five around 1840. He soon became prominent in local scientific and educational circles and published a Universalist journal, *The Primitive Expounder*. By 1843 he had become convinced that communal living would remedy society's greed and oppression.

He campaigned for Fourierism in his journal and on

December 14, 1843 called a convention to form a Michigan phalanx. Fifty-six delegates from Wayne, Oakland, Washtenaw, Genesee, Jackson, Eaton, Calhoun and Kalamazoo counties met at a schoolhouse near Jackson. Three days of debates yielded a rough constitution. The phalanx would be called Alphadelphia — first brotherhood.

Of three potential sites for Alphadelphia, Schetterly preferred a plat on the Kalamazoo River just west of Galesburg. He arrived there on December 23 to inspect the land. Galesburg area pioneers responded en masse to his persuasive rhetoric. On December 27, Schetterly wrote his fellow Fourierists that in Galesburg "an ardor now exists among the people in this place for entering into association which never can be cooled until their wishes shall have been realized".

The Fourierists reconvened in Bellevue on January 3, 1844 to perfect their constitution. The finished document contained a number of liberal provisions. Religious and political opinions of members were to be inviolate. Any who became ill would be provided for out of the common good. The labor and skill of male and female members were to be considered equal. All children would receive free education.

The Association worked something like a stock venture. Members relinquished their land, tools, personal effects, etc., which were appraised by Schetterly and converted into shares. All members labored eight hours a day at a suitable task and received a uniform wage.

By May 1844, more than 1,300 persons had become Alphadelphians. The Association purchased 2,814 acres of land at a cost of $32,000. The Alphadelphia domain on the Kalamazoo River hummed like a gigantic beehive that spring. Farmers, millwrights, machinists, furnacemen, printers, mechanics and skilled paper and cloth makers plied their trade for the good of all. The

Alphadelphians dug a millrace, set up a saw mill and erected a two-story "mansion" 20 feet by 200 feet in size.

By the following year, a wagon shop, blacksmith's forge and barns had been added. The brotherhood sold hides, baskets, grain and livestock and the first year's efforts showed a profit. The future looked bright for Kalamazoo County's Utopia. But aspects of basic human nature emerged. The leadership wrangled, and lack of privacy and the eccentricities of some jarred on others' nerves. What's more, as one old Alphadelphian later recalled: "Too many large families, poor and hungry, who could do no work, or were incapable of supporting themselves, got among us and were a continual expense — a hole in the meal bag from first to last."

Alphadelphia struggled on into 1848, then disbanded as each member tried to salvage something. Kalamazoo County purchased the site of the "mansion for a poor farm. Today it is River Oaks County Park.

Disillusioned with his fling with socialism, Schetterly secured a job with the federal government as lighthouse keeper at Grand Traverse Bay.

The Railroad that Led to Freedom

"Aunt" Laura Haviland of Adrian, famed underground railroad conductor.

The lumber wagon loaded with runaway slaves rumbled up to the front of Erastus Hussey's Battle Creek home. The conductor had driven through most of the night to make the 16 miles from the underground railroad station at Climax. His passengers climbed down from the wagon, stiff and sore from the jolting ride. A slave woman who had been there about a week waiting for the next shipment to the east busied herself helping Mrs. Hussey with her morning chores.

Suddenly she screamed, ran to the new arrivals and clasped a young girl to her chest. It was her own daughter whom she had not seen in 10 years. During the 1840s, when Michigan's underground railroad operated at its peak, many similiar episodes rivaled *Uncle Tom's Cabin* in pathos and adventure. Erastus Hussey said that he "could fill a book with such incidents."

Hussey, like so many others who made history, never got around to writing his book. But in 1885, Charles Barnes interviewed him about his experiences. Hussey remembered the beginnings of the underground railroad in 1840. Levi Coffin, a Quaker from Cincinnati, organized the system to spirit runaway slaves across the Ohio River and into Canada, beyond the reach of slave hunters. Other Quakers, enthusiastic abolitionists, operated most of the stations which were located 15 or 16 miles apart. Runaways traveled under cover of darkness and, during the day, hid and received meals at one of the stations.

John Cross, a Quaker from Indiana, established a route through Michigan. He appointed Hussey the conductor at Battle Creek in 1840. Within a month after accepting the position, which each conductor funded entirely out of his own pocket, the first two fugitives arrived in Battle Creek. Over the next two decades, until 1863 when Lincoln's Emancipation Proclamation freed all slaves still in the Confederacy, Hussey sheltered and fed over 1,000 runaways.

The underground railroad routes from Indiana and Illinois joined at a Quaker settlement in Cass County's Calvin Township, near Cassopolis. A number of Quaker families had settled there in the 1830s. In the 1840s, a group of free Blacks, originally from North Carolina, and other freed slaves joined them. Zachariah Shugart operated the underground railroad station in the Quaker settlement, and Parker Osborn was the agent at Cassopolis.

Shugart frequently conveyed loads of six to twelve runaways to the next station, Dr. Nathan Thomas's residence in Schoolcraft. Thomas's wife, Pamela, remembered many evenings when "after my little ones were asleep and I thought the labor of the day over, Friend Shugart would drive up with a load of hungry people to be fed and housed for the night." The Thomas home, currently under renovation by the Schoolcraft Historical Society, also housed over 1,000 runaway slaves over the years. It is one of the few documented underground railroad stations still standing.

William Gardner ran a station near Climax, and the next stop was Hussey's major depot at Battle Creek. Other documented stations were at Marshall, Albion, Parma, three stations at Jackson, Michigan Center, Leoni, Grass Lake, Francisco (a Jackson County ghost town), Dexter and Scio, a small village in Washtenaw County. Guy Beckely, editor of an abolitionist newspaper, *The Signal of Liberty*, ran the station at Ann Arbor. At Ypsilanti the route veered away from the Michigan Central Railroad to Plymouth and then ran along the River Rouge via Swartsburg to Detroit.

Another route from Ohio ran through Adrian. "Aunt" Laura Haviland, a Quaker teacher who helped found the first antislavery society in Michigan in 1832, became a famous operative on the underground railroad. She made dozens of forays into Ohio and Indiana conducting slaves through Michigan to Canada. She became so notorious that slaveholders put a $3,000 reward on her head.

An organization known as the Detroit Vigilance Committee took charge of slaves who arrived in the "City of the Straits." The hayloft of an old livery stable at the corner of State and Griswold usually held runaways waiting to be ferried across the river. Antislavery Detroiters formed the Refugee Home Society in 1851 and established a settlement for runaway slaves in Sandwich Township, south of Windsor, Ontario. The following year the Vigilance Committee moved 1,200 fugitives across the Detroit River.

In the early 1840s, underground railroad conductors practiced great secrecy. Small groups traveled only at night and, during the daytime, hid in attics, cellars or barns. Hussey remembered a common password used by slaves to locate a safe house, "can you give shelter and protection to one or more persons." But as more and more runaways began pouring into Michigan, some fugitives got careless. Lyman Goodnow, who guided a young runaway named Caroline from Wisconsin over the Michigan Central route in 1844, remembered seeing a gang of 32 escaped slaves openly traveling between Battle Creek and Marshall.

Information about Michigan antislavery activities eventually reached southern slave owners. A band of slave hunters from Bourbon County, Kentucky, the origin of some runaway slaves who had settled in Cass and Calhoun Counties, made a foray into Michigan in 1847. Zachariah Shugart and nine white guards marched 45 runaways from Cass County to Hussey's sanctuary in Battle Creek. But the slave hunters caught nine others. Before they could make their getaway, however, a crowd of local citizens armed with clubs and guns forced the Kentuckians to go to Cassopolis to prove their ownership of the Blacks before the court. A Circuit Court

Commissioner from Berrien County heard the case, found against the Kentuckians, and the runaways were hurried away on the underground railroad.

A similar raid occurred in Marshall. Adam Crosswhite, a runaway slave, and his family had settled in a Black community on the outskirts of town. A young Kentucky lawyer and three or four slave hunters seized the Crosswhite family. A rifle shot alerted local abolitionists who prevented their escape. The Kentuckians were arrested for assult and battery, and again the unguarded slaves disappeared on the underground railroad.

However, after several years of litigation, the Crosswhite and Cass County cases were overturned, and the participants paid Kentucky slave owners several thousand dollars damages for the loss of their "property."

Kentucky statesman Henry Clay also cited these Michigan incidents in support of the Fugitive Slave Law which went into effect in 1850 and helped bring on the Civil War.

Branded!

Captain Jonathan Walker, the man with the branded hand.

The red-hot branding iron sizzled as it bit deep into human flesh. A wisp of smoke drifted from the tiny Florida jail cell. It was 1844, and Captain Jonathan Walker had just been meted a portion of the sentence handed down by a federal court. To his dying day, he would carry the brand burned into his right palm: SS, for slave stealer.

Born in Harwich, Massachusetts in 1799, Walker left home at the age of seventeen to follow the life of a sailor. Long ocean voyages in sailing vessels brought adventure and danger. In 1818, while on a cruise to the Indian Ocean, he became desperately ill. Crew members marooned him on a small island where natives nursed him back to health. Twice he narrowly escaped drowning, and in 1824 he suffered a near fatal bout with yellow fever in Havana. He lived to become captain of a fishing vessel.

In the early 1830s Walker accompanied his friend, the famous abolitionist Benjamin Lundy, to Mexico in an effort to establish a colony for fugitive slaves. In 1835 when his boat ran ashore near the Mexican border, pirates attacked, wounded Walker, left him for dead, and made off with the boat and everything in it. But Walker survived, built another vessel and engaged in the shipping trade along the southern coast.

Around 1840, Walker accepted a contract to build a section of a projected railroad in Florida. He employed several slaves who ate at the same table and took part in Walker's family life; a friendship blossomed. In 1844, Walker set out in an open boat with seven slaves in an attempt to reach sanctuary in the British-owned Bahamas. Unfortunately, after they had rounded the Florida Cape, Walker was overcome by the intense tropical heat. His passengers knew nothing of navigation, and the tiny vessel drifted at the mercy of the winds and waves.

The crew of a passing sloop rescued the hapless band and conveyed them to Key West. Few crimes more infuriated hotheaded slaveholders than aiding and abetting their runaway property. Authorities chained Walker in the hold of a steamer which transported him to Pensacola for trial.

Walker lay shackled to the damp floor of a filthy jail cell for four months awaiting trial. Finally, a U.S. marshal hauled the emaciated prisoner before a U.S. District Court. Tried and convicted of slave stealing, the Court sentenced Walker to be branded on the right hand with the letters "SS," to stand in the pillory for one hour and a year of imprisonment and a heavy fine.

Walker's branding would be the only sentence ever so issued by a federal court. The authorities had a good deal of trouble in locating a blacksmith who would fashion a branding iron to be used on humans. The artisan who finally made the tool would not permit it to be heated for the branding at his forge. Walker was placed in the stocks in the courthouse square where a crowd pelted him with rotten eggs for an hour. Then a U.S. marshal chained him to the bars of his cell and administered the branding.

Walker languished eleven more months in the Pensacola jail with a heavy chain riveted to his leg. Finally, influential Northern friends raised money for his fine, and in the summer of 1845 he was released.

Walker's vicissitudes only served to increase the fervor of his antislavery activities. Returning to Massachusetts, he published an account of his experiences in 1846. He became a noted abolitionist speaker, traveling around the country to deliver stirring appeals. At a large gathering in Waltham, Massachusetts in August 1845, he vowed that "as long as life remained that branded hand should be raised against slavery." The climax of his many speeches came when he raised his right hand over his head to display the SS branded there.

Poet John Greenleaf Whittier, author of many verses that have become part of American culture, was also active in the antislavery movement. Inspired by Walker's experiences, he penned "The Branded Hand" in 1846. Whittier wrote:

> Then lift that manly right hand,
> bold ploughman of the wave!
> Its branded palm shall prophesy,
> "Salvation to the Slave!"
> Hold up its fire-wrought language,
> that whoso reads may feel
> His heart swell strong within him,
> his sinews change to steel.

Noted Black orator Frederick Douglass remembered Walker and his branded hand as "one of the few atrocities of slavery that roused the justice and humanity of the North to a death struggle with slavery."

When Abraham Lincoln signed the Emancipation Proclamation in 1863, Walker felt that his life work had been accomplished. He purchased a few acres at Lake Harbor on Black Creek just south of Muskegon and with his wife operated a small fruit farm. Walker's antislavery activities had been practically forgotten, and, modest and reserved, he led an unobtrusive life. In 1877, his health began to fail, and the couple was nearly destitute. Henry H. Holt of Muskegon launched a fund raising campaign. He circulated articles about Walker in newspapers across the country and sold photographs of his branded hand for $1.00. This appeal brought a generous response, including a contribution from Whittier.

When Walker died on April 30, 1878, Whittier corresponded with William Lloyd Garrison and other veterans of the antislavery crusade. The Rev. Photius Fisk, a U.S. Navy chaplain from Boston, paid for and shipped a 10-foot high granite obelisk to be erected over Walker's grave. One side of the staff contains a stanza from Whittier's poem and the other a carving of the branded hand.

The monument was placed near the entrance to Muskegon's Evergreen Cemetery. An estimated crowd of 6,000 turned out at the unveiling ceremonies on August 1, 1878. Local steamer and railroad lines made special excursion runs for the event. Today the weathered monument stands as a shrine to one man's courage in helping to set his fellow Americans free. As Whittier wrote:

And thy unborn generations,
as they tread our rocky strand.
Shall tell with pride the story of
their father's Branded Hand.

Wooden Shoes in the Wilderness

Rev. Albertus C. Van Raalte, founder of Holland.

The Reverend Albertus Van Raalte struggled through the waist-high snow. Indian missionary, the Reverend George Smith, and an Ottawa guide broke trail. Van Raalte, weakened by days of exploration in the dense wilderness of northern Allegan and Ottawa counties, could hardly lift his snowshoes. At times he could make no more than fifty paces before stopping to rest. But even as he rested, Van Raalte scooped through the snow to examine the quality of the underlying soil.

The Dutch pastor liked what he found. The thick growth of virgin hardwood indicated a fertile soil, and the timber would be ideal for fine furniture manufacturing. The tempering influence of nearby Lake Michigan would permit fruit growing. The unsettled land around the mouth of the Black River could be purchased cheaply. Perhaps most importantly, the river lay approximately halfway between the more developed Kalamazoo and Grand rivers where, upstream, Kalamazoo and Grand Rapids offered markets. Yet the Black River site was isolated enough to allow a theocratic Dutch colony to mature without the interference of the ungodly.

On New Years Day 1847, as local Ottawas marked the holiday by musket fire, Van Raalte selected the site for the city that would be known as Holland.

Conditions in the Netherlands were ripe for a mass migration to America. Like the Pilgrim fathers three centuries before, seceders from the state-sanctioned Reformed Church were persecuted. Deteriorating economic conditions brought about by the Dutch manufacturers' failure to compete with English producers were coupled with onerous taxes on food. Unemployment was widespread. In 1845-46, the potato blight that had such a severe effect on Ireland also eliminated this staple foodstuff in Holland.

Van Raalte, a 36-year-old pastor from the province of

Overijsel, led 100 followers to emigrate to the land of opportunity on September 24, 1846. They sailed on the "Southerner" from Rotterdam and, seven weeks later, arrived in New York City. Initially, Van Raalte planned to plant his colony in Wisconsin. The immigrants journeyed to Detroit via Albany and Buffalo and prepared to take a steamer up Lake Huron and through the Mackinac Straits to eastern Wisconsin. But the Straits had already frozen over, ending the shipping season.

Van Raalte found temporary employment in Detroit for his countrymen and took the Michigan Central Railroad west to the end of the line, Kalamazoo. There he met M.I. Coit and the Reverend Ova P. Hoyt, a Presbyterian minister. They and others, eager to secure for Michigan a better share of the settlers that had been bypassing the state for western lands, promoted local advantages. They convinced Van Raalte that western Michigan with its established population, "better educated, more religious and more enterprising people" than in Wisconsin, would be an ideal location for his colony.

They introduced Van Raalte to Judge John R. Kellogg of Allegan, who was knowledgeable about available lands in western Michigan. He suggested sites near Ada in Kent County, farther east in Ionia County and north of the Rabbit River in Allegan County. Kellogg guided Van Raalte along narrow Indian trails on an inspection tour from Allegan to the Old Wing Mission located in northern Allegan County's Fillmore Township. The Reverend George N. Smith, a Congregationalist clergyman, had established this mission in 1838. He resided in a wooden frame structure. He, his wife and Isaac Fairbanks sought to acculturate local tribesmen in white men's ways. Smith and Fairbanks led Van Raalte northwest into Ottawa County along an Indian trail to Black Lake where he determined to found his colony.

Van Raalte continued his reconnaissance of the wilderness until January 11 and then conducted legal research at Grand Haven, the Ottawa county seat. Returning to Detroit, then the state capital, he began purchasing land. He used some $10,000 of his own money realized from the sale of his brick and tile factory in Overijsel and borrowed funds from Americans proud of their Dutch heritage. Van Raalte bought some land at government prices of $1.25 an acre and other plats for back taxes, as low as 600 acres at $11.68. He also purchased 3,000 acres for $7,000 from New York City owners.

In early February, Van Raalte sent out a vanguard of six families to prepare the site for later arrivals. The women and children stayed in Allegan as the men made their way to headquarters at Old Wing Mission. By February 23, the colonists, with help from the Indians, had chopped out a road and constructed their first log house. Their families joined them from Allegan and brought news that additional parties of Hollanders were en route. Shelter and food to survive the tough winter became a serious problem. They were unused to American ways of building and ill supplied and equipped. Construction of dwellings proceeded slowly. The Dutch pioneers also had an unfortunate habit of felling trees on top of already completed cabins until they learned lumberjack skills.

They also got in trouble with the local Indians on several occasions. For example, they appropriated dressed venison found hanging from trees. Indian owners demanded restitution from Van Raalte, and he paid out of his own pocket. The worst offense occurred later in the year. During the spring, the Indians planted corn and bean fields and then left for their traditional hunting grounds in Berrien County. Assuming that they had deserted for good, the Hollanders assigned the Indian fields to newly arrived immigrants. When the tribe returned in the fall for harvesting, they found their crop lands overrun with Dutch settlers. Van Raalte attempted to resolve the problem but failed to completely satisfy the Indians. In 1849, the last of the local Indians moved with Smith to a new mission site near Northport in Leelanau County.

Most colonists survived the winter of 1847, but the summer brought worse problems. Weakened by poor foods and insufficient shelter, many fell victim to malaria spread by the hordes of mosquitoes that infested the undrained swamps. Others died of dysentery or of the smallpox epidemic introduced by new arrivals. Medical facilities were almost nonexistent. So many parents died that Van Raalte erected an orphanage.

Fortunately, the winter of 1847-48 proved mild, and, by the Spring of 1848, what the first colonists remembered as the "bitter days" had passed. More settlers continued to arrive from the old country and by 1860, Holland's population numbered 1,991. A fire that destroyed half the city in 1871 served only to cement a more tightly knit community. Unlike so many other American Utopian experiments that failed, Holland was there to stay.

Michigan, Michigan: City in the Forest

Lansing's first state capitol building constructed in 1847.

A smudge from huge piles of burning trees hung heavy over the newly created town of Michigan, Michigan. Teams of workmen chopped at hardwood giants, grubbed out the underbrush and graded pretentiously wide avenues. The state legislature had voted to establish the new state capital in the heart of a dense forest and all must be in readiness by Christmas 1847 for the next legislative session. One morning in the spring of 1847, most of the pioneers from Ingham County's Lansing Township assembled for a mammoth work party. The women piled tables heavy with food as the men labored to raise the frame of the new Capitol building, pausing occasionally to take a snort out of the whiskey jugs that always circulated freely at frontier raisings.

Detroit had been the seat of Michigan's government since territorial days. But the first state constitution drawn up in 1835 had stipulated that a "permanent" capital was to be selected by the legislature in 1847. Detroit continued to be the major metropolis of Michigan, but it was not centrally located, and its proximity to Canada left it open to military invasion. Perhaps more importantly, as settlers had established thriving communities across the peninsula, and the population distribution had shifted away from Wayne County, so too had the political power. By 1847, with outstate legislators in a majority, the political issue was not whether the capital should be relocated but which community would receive the plum.

Advocates from Jackson, Ann Arbor, Marshall and many smaller communities lobbied in support of their relative merits. The state House appointed a select committee to recommend a site. But the committee soon reached a deadlock and issued three separate reports. George Throop, chairman from Wayne County, quite naturally urged that the capital remain in Detroit. John

D. Pierce of Marshall, who had helped found the state's progressive school system, advanced his community's attractions. Ann Arbor and Jackson, Pierce maintained, were not only too far east, but each had already received its share of "public patronage" in the form of the University of Michigan and the state penitentiary.

Lastly, Enos Goodrich, from Genesee County, thought any city on the Michigan Central Railroad, which included Jackson, Ann Arbor and Marshall, too far south of the geographical center of the state to have "the permanence contemplated by the constitution." Some locale to the north would stimulate development in that region as well as swell state coffers through sale of state-owned lands.

Goodrich and a number of legislators from Livingston and Genesee counties formed a secret organization they called the "Northern Rangers" to advance their sectional interests. They were joined by James Seymour, an entrepreneur from Genesee County who had recently constructed a mill near what would become Lansing. Seymour wrote a letter to the legislators offering to supply free land for the new Capitol building and to erect temporary structures nearby for use until the permanent buildings were ready.

He further promoted his tract by placing a map of Michigan on every legislator's desk. The maps had been embellished with a red star marking Lansing Township and lines drawn to prominent Michigan cities showing distances. Clearly, Lansing Township was not only centrally located, but as Seymour described, possessed abundant water power potential, a fertile soil and rich hardwood forests. Seymour neglected to mention the many tamarack swamps infested with malarial mosquitoes or that the only roads to the place were Indian trails.

The House voted for 13 different sites during early February 1847. Ann Arbor, Dexter, Eaton Rapids,

Grand Blanc, Marshall, Jackson, Detroit and Byron in Shiawassee County went down to defeat. Then, Joseph H. Kilbourne of Ingham County introduced the dark horse candidate. Surprisingly, Lansing Township passed by a decisive vote of 48-17. The House Bill ran into problems in the Senate whose confused members voted 51 times in one day alone. Finally, on March 9, the bill passed the Senate, and Acting Governor William L. Greenly signed it into law on March 16, 1847.

The Legislature came up with the redundant appellation Michigan, Michigan for the new state capital (it was renamed Lansing in April,1848), and Governor Greenly appointed three commissioners to travel to Lansing Township and select the exact site. From Jackson, the nearest rail terminal, the commissioners journeyed for three days through the thick forest to Lansing Township. At Mason they built a raft to get across the swollen Sycamore Creek.

Upon their arrival, they were immediately besieged by local landowners offering inducements to get the capital on their tracts. Instead, the commissioners selected section 16, a square mile of land. The proceeds from the sale of section 16 of each Michigan township, sometimes called school sections, were allocated for school funding. The statutory price in 1847 was $4 an acre, higher than other government land. Hence, section 16 of Lansing Township had not been purchased.

Interestingly enough, while the bill designating Lansing Township as the new capital was being debated, A.L. Williams, a senator from Shiawassee County, overheard some other legislators plotting to buy Lansing's section 16 as a speculation. He informed Governor Greenly, who sent a letter to the State Land Commissioner at Marshall to withdraw the section from sale. Local tradition has it that an agent sent to buy the section rode on the same train that carried the governor's letter. The train was delayed and arrived in Marshall after the land office had closed for the day. But the letter that foiled the plot was delivered to the commissioner's home. As a result, sale of lots in Lansing netted the state school system more than $100,000 instead of $2,560.

The town of Michigan boomed in 1847 as speculators and entrepreneurs rushed to stake out their claims. Meanwhile a small army of workmen labored to transform the wilderness into a state capital. The handsome new 60 by 100-foot Greek revival Capitol building, surmounted by a tin cupola, stood complete in time for the legislative session of 1848. Lansing's first Capitol building stood in the middle of a square one block southeast of the present structure which replaced it in 1879. By then, Lansing had become Michigan's capital in stature as well as name.

Under The Oaks at Jackson

Founders of the Republican Party gathered for a 50th anniversary celebration in Jackson.

The Michigan Central locomotive chugged to a stop at the Jackson depot. A cloud of steam hissed from the engine, as the cars disgorged a stream of passengers. There were newspaper editors, doctors, farmers, artisans of all types, well-dressed lawyers and roughly-clad frontiersmen. All had one thing in common. It was the morning of July 6, 1854, and they had come to give birth to the Republican Party.

Delegates had begun arriving the previous day. One party of twenty from the Saginaw Valley had ridden over one hundred miles on horseback. By the morning of the sixth, over 3,000 strangers surged through Jackson's streets. Jackson, a prosperous village where the state census taker had recently counted 3,326 inhabitants, had no structure able to accommodate the throng. Nevertheless, as many delegates as could squeezed into the city hall, and the convention was called to order at 10:30 a.m.

Levi Baxter of Jonesville was appointed temporary chairman of the meeting. Baxter, a consummate politician flush from a legislation coup in which he had caused the Michigan Southern Railroad to be kinked four miles to the north so that it reached his hometown, delivered a stirring oration and then appointed a committee on permanent organization. Meanwhile, workmen hastily erected a large platform and rough plank seats in a grove of ancient oak trees.

Slavery was the issue that had aroused this Jackson convention. Moreover, extension of slavery to the west had put the old American political powers in a state of flux. The Missouri Compromise of 1820 had admitted Missouri into the Union as a slave state but prohibited the entrance of other slave states from the territory to the west that lay north of Missouri's southern border. But the acquisition of large tracts of western land during the Mexican War of 1846-48 reopened the issue. The

Compromise of 1850 temporarily quieted the strife, but the Kansas-Nebraska Act of 1854 again embroiled the nation in controversy. The Kansas-Nebraska Act applied the concept of "popular sovereignty" to the western territories, that is, the settlers of each incipient state could decide for themselves the status of slavery.

Michigan's premier statesman, Lewis Cass, had originated the principle of popular sovereignty in 1847. Opposition to it by Democrats, antislavery Whigs and others who seceded from their parties to create the Free Soil Party had cost Cass the presidential election of 1848. Despite Cass's popularity in his home state, Michigan became a hotbed for the Free Soil Party. The Dred Scott decision, which legalized slavery in the territories, and "Bleeding Kansas," where pro and antislavery advocates slaughtered each other, further enflamed the national mood.

During the spring of 1854, Michigan Whigs, Free Soilers, Abolitionists and "anti Nebraska" Democrats held a number of conferences to discuss forming a political union in opposition to the proslavery tendencies of the regular Democratic Party. The Free Soil state committee issued a call for a mass convention to be held in Kalamazoo on June 21, 1854. Clearly the Whig Party was dying, and many of Michigan's Whig-oriented newspapers campaigned vigorously for a new fusion party.

Over 1,000 delegates attended the Kalamazoo convention at which they drew up antislavery resolutions and determined to join forces to create a new political party. Soon, newspapers across the state called for a mass convention at Jackson on July 6, 1854 "to concentrate the popular sentiment of this state against the encroachment of the slave power."

Following the morning session in Jackson City Hall, the crowd of delegates reassembled in an oak grove near the present intersection of Second and Washington streets. It was a beautiful spot. The ground, "covered with a thick sward of grass," sloped gently away from the mound where the speaker's stand had been erected. It was a bright sunshiny day and the 100 old oaks in the grove offered welcome shade. The Jackson brass band regaled the sea of delegates with patriotic airs, and the meeting came to order.

The Committee on Permanent Organization announced it had selected David S. Walbridge of Kalamazoo as president of the party. Then leaders from Michigan's four congressional districts selected three electors from each district to form a committee to develope a "platform of principles." While this committee met, prominent orators delivered speeches to the delegates.

Zachariah Chandler of Detroit, who would become Michigan's first Republican senator in 1857, delivered a stirring appeal. "Misfortunes make strange bedfellows. I see before me Whigs, Democrats and Free Soilers, all mingling together to rebuke a great national wrong."

Another popular presentation came from Lewis Clark of Sandwich, Ontario. The model for George Harris in *Uncle Tom's Cabin*, Clark related how he and his family had been sold on the auction block and suffered much cruelty before escaping to Canada. His "earnest, plain unlettered statement" received a loud ovation from the assembled antislavery activists.

The Committee on Resolutions announced that a name had been selected for the new party - Republican. Then Jacob Howard of Detroit read the first Republican platform: "Resolved, that the institution of slavery, except in the punishment of crime, is a great moral, social and intellectual evil..." The platform received "three hearty cheers by the multitude," and the meeting adjourned until a nominating committee could develope a list of candidates.

The delegates reconvened on the public square at 7

p.m. to hear the first Republican state ticket: Kinsley S. Bingham of Livingston County would run for governor and candidates for the other state offices were representatives of the various factions that had combined to form the Republican Party.

Bingham and the entire Republican ticket swept the election in November 1856. The Republican Party movement spread rapidly across the northern states. The party's first presidential candidate, John C. Fremont, was defeated in 1856, but Abraham Lincoln led the Republicans to triumph in 1860. Michigan remained a bastion of the Republican Party until the election of 1932.

The King of Beaver Island

James Jesse Strang, King of Beaver Island.

The King of Beaver Island strode calmly toward the wharf at St. James Harbor. It was a mid-June evening in 1856, and the monarch was preoccupied with thought. Ruling the spiritual and civil lives of some 2,600 Mormon subjects who dwelt within the 53-square-mile kingdom located 30 miles offshore from Charlevoix required concentration. Or perhaps King Strang mulled over some domestic squabble instigated by one of his four pregnant wives.

Suddenly, as Strang stepped upon the dock, two disgruntled followers appeared behind him. Alexander Wentworth cooly cocked a long-barreled "horse pistol" and shot his king in the side of the head. Strang pitched forward, and Wentworth and Thomas Bedford fired two more rounds into his face and back. As the assassins ran by, Strang grabbed Bedford's leg and Bedford then beat him unconscious with his pistol butt.

Wentworth and Bedford jumped into a waiting launch, and the crew, who had calmly watched the shooting, rowed them to the U.S. Navy steamer *Michigan* anchored in the harbor. A group of Mormons carried their wounded leader to a nearby house.

Born March 21, 1813, James Jesse Strang had grown up in western New York state. His appearance gave little indication of royalty. He was short, red-haired and had an abnormally large head. But his piercing eyes and deep vibrant voice indicated an inner strength.

He early developed grandiose expectations. When 19 he chided himself in diary entries for his lack of success. He expected "to rival Caesar or Napoleon." A few months later he spent a day "trying to contrive some plan" to marry the future Queen Victoria, then 12 years old.

Strang became a lawyer at the age of 23 and perfected a hypnotic oratorical ability. But he found the legal profession too tame and immigrated west to Wisconsin

Territory in 1843. There, a Mormon apostle, whose shrill pulpit exhortations rattled window panes, converted Strang. He journeyed to Nauvoo, Illinois, then the Mormon capital, to be personally baptized by church founder Joseph Smith. Soon ordained an elder, Strang was sent on a mission to Wisconsin to scout out a new home for the beleaguered Saints.

When Joseph and Hyrum Smith were murdered by a mob, the Mormon church was thrown into chaos. As Brigham Young scrambled for control, a number of rival successors emerged. Strang threw his hat into the ring when he produced an apocryphal letter from Joseph Smith endorsing him as the true heir. The church excommunicated Strang, but he established a rival Zion at Voree in southeastern Wisconsin.

The Voree community gained divine sanction when Strang miraculously discovered a set of ancient tablets under conditions remarkably similar to Joseph Smith's experience near Palmyra, New York in 1827. Through the aid of magic peep stones, Strang translated the hieroglyphics into *The Book of the Law of the Lord*, a supplement to *The Book of Mormon.*

Brigham Young sought refuge from gentile persecution by leading his followers to Utah in 1846. Strang faced with similar problems, located an ideal sanctuary nearer to civilization - Beaver Island.

Strang and four companions made a scouting foray to the island in 1847 and found much to their liking. The island was sparsely inhabited by Irish fishermen and Indian traders who made a good living by swapping for fish a special blend of watered-down whiskey flavored with chewing tobacco and red pepper. Strang planted a small colony of people on the island. By the summer of 1849, a mass exodus of Strangite Mormons had arrived in the land of milk and honey.

Industrious Mormons carved farmsteads out of the interior wilderness, built roads and began acquiring control of the entire island as well as the choicest fishing grounds. They renamed the harbor and settlement St. James and bestowed biblical names on local geographic features. Needless to say, friction developed between the Saints and the fiesty Irish fishermen they had surplanted.

Some property was purchased legitimately, but Strang also appointed a sheriff who issued certificates of sale for land belonging to the government or absent owners. When President Millard Fillmore failed to grant his petition for title to all the uninhabited islands in Lake Michigan, Strang announced that God had given the property to him and his people.

Strang revealed this startling fact at his coronation on July 8th 1850. During an imposing pageant out of medieval history, the crimson-robed Strang walked solemnly into a hewn-log tabernacle where a former actor turned saint placed a crown on his auburn head. Henceforth, July 8th, King's Day, replaced July 4th as Beaver Island's national day of celebration.

As the Mormon population of the island multiplied, the displaced Irish grew more hostile. Raiders from their new headquarters on Mackinac Island waylaid Mormon fishermen, broke into households and molested women. The Mormons struck back, and both sides committed atrocities.

Eastern newspapers publicized the bitter feuding and usually depicted the Mormons as a band of pirates. During a visit to Detroit, President Fillmore learned of the Beaver Island kingdom and ordered Strang arrested. Strang surrendered himself, conducted his own defense at the trial in Detroit and won an acquittal. In 1853 he rigged the local election to win a seat in the Michigan legislature.

King Strang's rule was that of a benevolent despot guided by divine wisdom. Periodic visions enacted his personal prejudices into law. He reversed an earlier stand against polygamy when he fell in love with a teen-aged schoolmarm. Yet his legal code proscribed death for adultery.

Strang established schools, set up a royal printing press, published a newspaper and wrote a variety of pamphlets. He prohibited alcohol, coffee, tea, tobacco, and gambling. The King decreed the national costume for women to be the pantaloon and short skirt ensemble popularized by Amelia Bloomer. Violators of Strang's code were subject to public flogging.

Thomas Bedford had been whipped by order of the King, reputedly for upholding his wife's refusal to don bloomers. Alexander Wentworth harbored a similar grievance. Aided by Gentile enemies, the pair took their revenge by shooting Strang. The *Michigan* conveyed the assassins to Mackinac Island for a hero's welcome. They were never brought to trial.

Suspecting another attack, the Saints moved their wounded King to Voree. The invasion came on July 5, 1856. A mob of drunken rowdies stormed the kingdom. They burned the tabernacle, sacked the printing office and roamed the island herding Mormon families at gunpoint to waiting transports. Within a few days some 2,600 men, women and children were ruthlessly evicted from their homes and cast ashore at various Great Lakes ports. Byron M. Cutcheon, a turn-of-the-century Michigan historian, termed July 5, 1856, "the most disgraceful day in Michigan history."

King Strang died of his wounds on July 9th 1856. Though able to converse until the end, he refused to name a successor. That spelled doom for the Strangite Mormon Church. Leaderless and scattered, the flock soon dispersed. But a few die-hards remained loyal, and as late as 1936, Michigan claimed 15 practicing Strangite Mormons.

Today, Beaver Island is the "most remote inhabited island in the Great Lakes." A permanent population of

350 people, predominantly of Irish descent, make a living by fishing, logging and catering to the tourist trade.

The original Mormon Print Shop Museum, a body of fascinating literature, and place names like the King's Highway, Lake Geneserath and Mount Pisgah are all that remain of King Strang's utopian dream, "the only kingdom ever to exist in the United States."

The Taming of the Sault

The rock-strewn shore at Sault Ste. Marie, ca. 1853.

White water, churning with whirlpools and cataracts, dashing spray high in the air, boiled and roared over a sandstone ledge thickly strewn with granite boulders, a half mile plug that holds the level of Lake Superior some 23 feet higher than Lake Huron, 45 miles downstream. Native Chippewa knew how to shoot the rapids in their frail birch-bark canoes, but no other craft could navigate the Sault (French for rapids) Ste. Marie. This furious stretch at the head of the St. Marys River, where the water drops 18 feet in a half mile, posed an impossible barrier to shipping on the only water route into Lake Superior.

The first attempt to tame the rapids came on the Canadian side in 1797. The Northwest Company constructed a small lock that enabled voyagers' canoes, heavily laden with furs, to bypass a portion of the rapids. But American raiders destroyed this site during the War of 1812, and British fur traders relocated elsewhere.

On the American side, an ancient portage path offered the traditional route around the rapids. Traders lugged canoes, bundles of furs and trade goods along the portage. In 1839, laborers dragged the schooner *Algonquin* around the rapids on greased rollers. That same year, the American Fur Company constructed a primitive strap iron railroad along the portage route and conveyed cargo in horse-drawn cars.

Michigan's initial experiment in building a canal at Sault Ste. Marie proved a fiasco. Governor Stephens T. Mason had promoted an ambitious plan for internal improvements in 1837, including three railroads and a canal around the St. Marys rapids. The state legislature authorized a $5 million loan for these projects.

The Board of Internal Improvements let bids in April 1838 for a canal 75 feet wide and 10 feet deep with three locks. A Buffalo firm won the contract, and in May 1839, contractor Aaron Weeks arrived at the Sault with a shipload of supplies and workmen. He commenced work by cutting across a millrace that had been constructed in 1823 to power the Fort Brady sawmill. When an officer from the fort ordered him to stop, Weeks refused, whereupon a contingent of U.S. troops drove the workers away at bayonet point. Apparently this was what Weeks actually wanted. He realized the firm had bid the job too low and was anxious to find some legal means to cancel the contract.

Michigan politicians made a lot of noise in congress over the federal government trampling on the rights of a sovereign state, but to little avail. Undaunted, Michigan spokesmen campaigned in congress not only for a right of way through Fort Brady but also for a federal appropriation to finance the canal. In 1840, Kentucky statesman Henry Clay made a speech against the canal bill remarking that it was "a work beyond the remotest settlement in the United States, if not in the moon," and the measure was defeated.

The Michigan Legislature continued its appeals to congress over the following decade. Due in part to the discovery of vast deposits of copper and iron in the Upper Peninsula during the 1840s, Congress finally approved a Sault canal bill on August 26, 1852. As a result, 750,000 acres of federal land in Michigan would be donated to the state to finance the project.

Charles T. Harvey, an employee of the Fairbanks Scale Company of Vermont, happened to be in the Sault when he learned of the bill. Realizing that the canal would open to the world the mineral resources of the U.P. in which his firm had invested, Harvey convinced his employers that he should devote his time to promoting the project.

Harvey hired an engineer to make a preliminary study of the site and with the help of two officials of the Michigan Central Railroad from Detroit succeeded in pushing a bill through the state Legislature on February 5, 1853. The contract was awarded to the St. Marys Falls Ship's Canal Company of New York made up of Fairbanks, the two Detroit railroad officials and other investors. It called for a lock 70 feet wide and 350 feet long, and the whole project was to be completed in two years. Harvey was also appointed by the governor as special agent to select the lands to be given to the contractor. He chose 140,000 acres in the U.P., including the site of the Calumet and Hecla copper mine, and over 600,000 acres of valuable northern Michigan timber lands.

Harvey turned from promotion to supervision of the construction work. He purchased horses, tools and supplies in Detroit, hired 400 laborers, loaded everything aboard a steamer and arrived at the Sault on June 1, 1853. The few laborers available in the Sault were antagonistic to the project because it would ruin their portaging trade. Consequently, Harvey had to import an army of workers that eventually numbered from 2,000 to 3,000. He sent agents to New York City who hired gangs of newly arrived Irish immigrants. Harvey constructed 50 shanties, similar to those used by lumberjacks. Fifty laborers ate and slept at each shanty. Far ahead of his time in work benefits, Harvey also maintained a hospital and doctor for his men.

Harvey faced an enormous challenge in completing the work on schedule. Should he fail, the choice land he had reserved as payment would likely be put back on the market. Over 3,000 kegs of dynamite were used to blast out the excavation. Bitter winter weather with temperatures of -30 degrees delayed progress. A cholera epidemic in 1854 filled the hospital with laborers. Harvey quickly ended a strike, during which over a thousand of his men marched around town, by cutting off food supplies at the shanties.

Despite these problems, the project appeared to be

nearing completion ahead of schedule. Then Harvey discovered two errors in the government surveys. A change in the level of Lake Superior required the hand chiseling of another foot of rock out of the entire channel. Even worse, a reef which showed on government charts as sand turned out to be solid rock. Harvey ingeniously devised a gigantic punch with which he pulverized the ledge.

On May 31, 1855, Harvey turned over his engineering marvel, the first ship canal in America, to the state of Michigan. A canal 5,400 feet long and 100 feet wide and two locks, each 350 feet long and 70 feet wide, that raised and lowered ships 18 feet had been completed at a cost of just under $1 million. On June 18, 1855, the steamer *Illinois* became the first ship to lock through.

Michigan operated the "state lock" on a toll basis until the federal government took over in 1881 and made passage free. The first lock was ultimately destroyed to make way for the much larger Poe lock that opened in 1896. Rebuilt in 1968, the Poe lock, the largest of four American locks, can accommodate freighters 100 feet wide and 1,000 feet long.

They Booed Lincoln in Kalamazoo

Abraham Lincoln as he appeared in the 1860 campaign.

The tall man mounted the speakers' platform that stood atop the ancient Indian mound in downtown Kalamazoo's Bronson Park. A worn coat and vest hung loosely on his gaunt frame, and his trousers barely reached his ankles. His huge gnarled hands grasped the podium as he began to address the crowd in a surprisingly shrill voice.

As Abraham Lincoln spoke, his sad homely face shone with passion and his grey eyes flashed. "The question is simply this: Shall slavery be spread into new territories, or not? This is the naked question."

That "naked question" had the entire country in ferment. The issue, in fact, had spurred the formation of the Republican Party in Jackson, Michigan on July 6, 1854.

Two years later, John Brown's raid and "Bleeding Kansas," where slaveholders and abolitionists massacred each other, swept national headlines. 1856 was an election year. In an era when Americans took their politics seriously, few were ambivalent on the issues.

The Republicans launched their first presidential campaign that year under the banner of "free speech, free press, free soil, free men and Fremont." The latter, colorful western adventurer John C. Fremont, ran against Democrat James Buchanan and Know Nothing Party candidate Millard Fillmore.

In early August, Republican newspapers across the state issued a call for a "Great Mass convention of the Republican Young Men of Michigan" to be held in Kalamazoo. On August 27, 1856, Republicans poured into Kalamazoo by train, wagon, horseback and on foot. Estimates varied between 8,000 and 30,000 people.

Hezekiah G. Wells, Kalamazoo attorney and chairman of the executive committee in charge of the meeting, had made sure the village was in readiness. A huge banner bearing the names of the Republican state and national nominees stretched across Michigan Avenue. Citizens decorated hotels, stores and private homes with gaily colored flags and bunting.

Thirty-one guns saluted dawn that day as contingents began arriving at the Michigan Central depot. Detroit, Ann Arbor, Jackson, Battle Creek, Grand Rapids, and Marshall sent bands. The Battle Creek Glee Club joined the hullabaloo with a rendition of a campaign air sung to the tune of the "Marsellaise," the French national anthem.

Delegates paraded from the depot to Bronson Park. Ladies from nearby Richland formed a procession with 31 women dressed in white to represent the sister states, and a lone woman symbolic of Kansas followed behind, shrouded in black. Throughout the village, "all Republican doors were open" to the visitors. To feed the throng, the committee erected a 100-foot-long table in the park. At noon, two tons of bread, 400 hams and corresponding quantities of beef, potatoes and coffee disappeared into hungry mouths.

Four platforms to accommodate the dozens of speakers had been erected in Bronson Park. Michigan sent her best orators. Lincoln, the only speaker from out of state, was an Illinois congressman, little known beyond his district. Wells had met him at a convention in Philadelphia and invited him to Kalamazoo. The only newspaper in the state that heralded his coming was the Battle Creek *Journal*, and it misspelled his first initial.

Lincoln was scheduled to speak at 2 p.m. He took the Michigan Central from Chicago, arrived in Kalamazoo at 1:32 and shouldered his way through the confusion to the rostrum. Lincoln's speech gave little hint of the eloquence he would display in the Gettysburg Address. He urged moderation and conciliation. But when Lincoln pleaded for compromise on the Kansas question, his audience howled and booed.

Hot-blooded abolitionists, in no mood for compromise, dominated this Republican gathering. Lincoln, the only "foreign speaker" on the program, was probably the least popular. Lincoln's calm impassioned reasoning, however, so impressed a reporter for the Kalamazoo *Gazette* that he devoted nearly half of his article to a favorable review of the speech. The *Gazette,* a Democratic journal, allotted only sarcastic mention to the other Republican orators.

Fortunately for posterity, the Republican-oriented Detroit *Advertiser* sent a reporter to cover the meeting. He had been trained in the shorthand technique invented by Sir Isaac Pitman. Lincoln's speech appeared practically verbatim in the *Advertiser's* August 29 issue.

Lincoln delivered over 50 speeches during the 1856 campaign, but his Kalamazoo talk is the only one that has survived. Lost and forgotten, it was rediscovered by a researcher in 1930.

Lincoln's Kalamazoo talk was to be the only speech he ever made in Michigan. Few in the audience that booed him in 1856 could have imagined that this unpopular stranger would lead the nation through its supreme trial - the Civil War.

"Come On You Wolverines!"

General George Armstrong Custer led the cavalry charge at the Battle of Aldie, Va. on June 17, 1863.

General George Armstrong Custer drew his long Spanish sabre, spurred his mount to the head of the 7th Michigan Cavalry Regiment and shouted "Come on you Wolverines!" He wore a black velvet uniform elaborately trimmed with gold lace on the sleeves and trouser seams. A crimson necktie hung from his collar. His shoulder-length, reddish-blond hair streamed from under a wide-brimmed hat turned down on one side in a rakish fashion. He was handsome, tall, lithe, and he rode ramrod straight in the saddle, like an aristocrat.

It was July 3, 1863, the third and decisive day of the Battle of Gettysburg. Custer had won promotion from captain to brigadier general for conspicuous bravery during a cavalry charge at the Battle of Aldie, Virginia the previous month. At 23 he was the youngest general in the Union Army. On June 29th, he had taken command of a brigade composed of the 1st, 5th, 6th and 7th Michigan Cavalry Regiments, organized in Grand Rapids and Detroit.

Initially the men disliked their flamboyant young commander. His strict enforcement of military discipline and aloof behavior toward older subordinant officers did not help matters. But the "boy general" began earning their respect through his bravery. The previous day he had led a company of cavalry in a charge against a superior force during which his horse was shot out from under him. Before July 3 was over the men of "Custer's Cavalry Brigade" would begin to idolize their leader and eventually even adopt his scarlet tie as their symbol.

The Battle of Gettsyburg had begun by accident when a Confederate infantry brigade in search of shoes blundered into a Union cavalry force near the small Pennsylvania farming community. The first two days of savage fighting, which pitted General Robert E. Lee's army against General George Meade's Army of the

Potomac, had brought no decisive victory. On the afternoon of July 3, following a furious artillery barrage, Lee launched 13,000 men, spearheaded by Major General Pickett's fresh division, against the Union positions. A mile-long line of Confederates marched in military precision across an open field to be slaughtered by Union artillery and musket fire.

Simultaneously, Lee ordered Major General J.E.B. Stuart to attack the Union rear with his heretofore nearly invincible cavalry. Stuart's force, jaded from ten days of furious fighting, was in no condition to battle Custer's brigade. They encountered Custer's men about five miles southeast of Gettysburg. Custer ordered the Fifth Michigan under Colonel Russell Alger to attack on foot. Owing to the superior fire power of their eight-shot Spencer repeating carbines, Alger's men pushed the Confederates back until, out of ammunition, the Michigan men retreated.

At that point Custer ordered the Seventh Michigan Cavalry to attack, inspiring them by example as he led the charge halfway across the field. The Confederate cavalry rallied, and the field was a swirling mass of blue and gray fighting hand to hand, mounted and on foot.

Suddenly an additional eight regiments of Stuart's cavalry appeared from the woods and began forming up for an attack. As Confederate Generals Wade Hampton and Fitzhugh Lee led the sabre charge, a Union battery poured a murderous barrage into their ranks. Against overwhelming odds the 5th, 6th, and 7th Michigan Cavalry Regiments struck the Confederate flanks. Then Custer led the 1st Michigan in a furious charge against the middle of the Confederate force. Yelling and slashing wildly, Custer's troopers cut through the long gray-coated column and Stuart's cavalry "gave way in a disorderly rout."

This "finest cavalry charge made during the Civil War" ended Stuart's threat. Had the Confederate cavalry broken through to attack Meade's practically undefended rear the crucial battle might well have ended in a Union defeat. As it was, it marked the beginning of the end for the Confederacy.

Custer's star, on the other hand, was on the ascendant. Born in New Rumley, Ohio in 1839, he moved to Monroe, Michigan at the age of 10 to live with his married half sister. He attended public school and a "Young Men's Academy" there. At the age of 16 he returned to Harrison County, Ohio, where he taught school at a salary of $26 a month and board.

In 1857 Custer received an appointment to West Point. Three days after graduating at the bottom of his class of 35 pupils, he participated in the disastrous First Battle of Bull Run. Custer proved himself a courageous leader during many subsequent battles. He also became one of the first Union officers to observe the enemy during combat from a hot air balloon. On Thanksgiving Day 1862 while on leave, Custer was formally introduced to Elizabeth Bacon, daughter of a Monroe judge. They were married at the Presbyterian Church in Monroe on February 9, 1864. Libbie Custer followed her husband to the front during the last year of the war and during his subsequent nine years of service on the western frontier.

Following its victory at the Battle of Gettysburg, Custer's Michigan Cavalry Brigade continued to distinguish itself as one of the most spirited and courageous units in the Union army. During almost continuous combat service it lost 524 troopers, more than any other Union cavalry brigade.

On September 30, 1864, Custer left his Michigan units to take command of the 3rd Cavalry Division. He won national fame for his heroic leadership and became one of General Philip Sheridan's most trusted commanders. Custer was promoted to major general on April 15, 1865.

Fearless, bold and inspiring, Custer was also very lucky. During the Civil War, eleven horses were shot out from under him, but he only received one slight wound himself. His luck, however, ran out at the Battle of the Little Big Horn on June 25, 1876.

From her home in Monroe, Libbie Custer defended her husband's memory until her death in 1933. Custer remains a controversial figure because of his Indian campaigns, but few discredit his heroic service during the Civil War.

The "Confederacy in Petticoats"

General Benjamin Pritchard, Union commander who captured Jefferson Davis.

The half dozen tents, dimly outlined by the first light of dawn, had been hastily pitched in the pine forest near Irwinsville, Georgia. A wisp of smoke from a dying campfire spiraled upward. Confederate President Jefferson Davis, his family, a few servants and several other Confederate officials lay fast asleep. It was May 10, 1865.

Lee had surrendered to Grant at Appomattox on April 9, but Davis had fled Richmond hoping to link up with General Kirby Smith, who still controlled the Trans-Mississippi Department, and thus continue the Confederacy.

Suddenly, the thud of horses' hooves shook the ground as blue-coated cavalrymen swept through the camp. Without firing a shot, Lt. Col. Benjamin Pritchard and a contingent of the 4th Michigan Cavalry had captured Davis.

Before Pritchard could secure his captives, a volley of musket fire rang out from where he had ordered a squad to surround the camp. He galloped to the scene, set up a skirmish line and began advancing on the force. But the opposing rifle fire did not sound like the Confederate weapons he had heard so often over the last three years "Cease fire," he called, and shouted to his opponents, "Who are you?" "First Wisconsin," they answered. In their eagerness to capture Davis, the two Union cavalry units had mistaken each other for the enemy and had engaged in a fire fight. Two members of the 4th Michigan Cavalry lay dead, a lieutenant was severely wounded and seven or eight men of the 1st Wisconsin Cavalry received wounds.

Meanwhile, Jefferson Davis had decided to make one last bid for freedom. A ruse seemed his only hope. Mrs. Davis called out to the guard for permission to let someone go for water.

A tall stooped-over figure in a cloak and a shawl

emerged from the tent carrying a water bucket. Arm in arm with another femininely dressed person they hurried toward the creek.

But Private Andrew Bee spied a pair of high boots with spurs under the cloak and called out. A trooper rode over and halted the two with a cocked rifle. The tall figure straightened up and angrily threw off the cloak and shawl. Jefferson Davis, the proud southern cavalier, had been caught sneaking away disguised as a woman.

Pritchard returned from the unfortunate fight with the 1st Wisconsin and proceeded to question Davis. Born in Nelson, Ohio in 1835, Pritchard had moved to Allegan, Michigan in 1856. Following graduation from the University of Michigan in 1860, he set up a law practice there. In the summer of 1862, Pritchard recruited 105 men, mostly from Allegan County, to form Company L of the 4th Michigan Calvary. The troops elected him their captain.

The 4th Michigan Cavalry won fame during almost constant combat service from October 1862 until the end of the war. In addition to prolonged scouting duty and forays against General Nathan Bedford Forrest's cavalry, it played an active role during the battles of Murfreesboro and the Chattanooga and Atlanta campaigns.

Pritchard proved a brave and efficient company commander. He led several cavalry charges into battle and gained "the reputation of being the best soldier in the regiment." In 1864 he was promoted directly from captain to lieutenant colonel in command of the regiment.

Gen. James Wilson, commander of Gen. Sherman's cavalry, selected his two best regiments to pursue the fleeing Jefferson Davis, the 4th Michigan Cavalry and the 1st Wisconsin Cavalry under Lt. Col. Henry Harnden. Unfortunately, the two crack units collided in battle.

The 4th Michigan marched its captives back to Macon. En route they met the remainder of the brigade equipped with a brass band. The band struck up "Yankee Doodle" and "Old John Brown" and the troops lining the road sang, "We'll hang Jeff Davis on a sour apple tree."

Pritchard also learned that President Andrew Johnson had posted a $100,000 reward for the capture of Davis as one of the Lincoln assassination conspirators. Three and a half years later, that sum was divided among Pritchard, Harnden, Wilson and their men.

Sensationalist Northern newspapers intensified Southern humiliation by embellishing Davis's escape attempt. They concocted the story that Davis wore a hoop skirt and ran headlines about the "confederacy in petticoats." P.T. Barnum added his own bit of humbug by exhibiting a tableau of Davis, so dressed, resisting the cavalrymen.

Davis, shackled and in solitary confinement at first, was imprisoned within Fortress Monroe, Virginia for two years. Finally, President Andrew Johnson pardoned Davis on Christmas 1868. Free but a broken man, Davis spent the rest of his life denying that he had acted dishonorably at the time of his capture. An autobiographical sketch he wrote just prior to his death in 1889 devoted more space to his capture than to his entire role as president of the Confederacy.

Benjamin Pritchard was promoted to brigidier general for his part in the capture. He returned to Allegan for a hero's welcome and a permanent place of honor in the town's memory, as the man who captured Jefferson Davis.

The Floating Inferno

The ill-fated Sultana overloaded with troops.

Faded blue uniforms hung loosely on their gaunt bodies. Weakened by months of starvation, disease and brutality in the infamous Confederate prison at Andersonville, Georgia and Cahaba, Alabama, many of the recently released soldiers that crowded the wharf at Vicksburg, Mississippi could hardly walk. Despite their condition, the men joked and bantered with each other. They were going home - back to loved ones in Indiana, Ohio and Michigan.

It was April 24, 1865. Lee had surrendered to Grant at Appomattox Court House on April 9th, and for all practical purposes, the war that had pitted brother against brother for four bloody years was over. Now the ex-prisoners waited anxiously at Vicksburg for transport up the Mississippi by river boat. The Sultana, a 1,719 ton side-wheeler built in 1863 for the lower Mississippi cotton trade, arrived from New Orleans that evening.

As the ship's engineer supervised some apparently routine repairs to the boilers, the troops streamed up the gangplank. The Sultana had taken on at New Orleans 75 cabin passengers and a cargo of 100 hogsheads of sugar, 60 horses and mules, and one crated 10-foot "man eating" alligator. She carried a crew of 85 and legally could only transport 376 passengers in all. Nevertheless, when she slowly pulled away from the wharf at Vicksburg, between 1,800 and 2,000 ex-prisoners of war and two companies of soldiers under arms had clambered aboard. The troops, for which the ship owners received a set fee of $5 per head, covered every square foot of space from the hurricane deck to the pilot house. Of the approximately 2,300 people on board, more than 250 were from Michigan.

To compound the situation, the Mississippi was in flood stage with an exceptionally strong current. The troops sprawled out on the sagging decks and cooked their own meals using hot water from the boilers as the Sultana slowly splashed upstream. Two days later, the vessel docked at Memphis. Some of the troops went ashore to stretch their legs and got so involved in sightseeing that they missed the boat. They little realized how lucky they were.

After additional repair work on one of the leaky boilers, the ship crossed the river to take on coal. A little after midnight on the 27th it left for Cairo, Illinois, where most of the soldiers were to disembark for rail travel home. About 2 a.m., as the overloaded vessel laboring against the strong current neared a cluster of islands known as the "Hen and Chickens," it happened.

A tremendous explosion, heard all the way back to Memphis, disintegrated half of the Sultana. The boilers, that had proved troublesome during the entire voyage, had blown up, hurling huge fragments of the superstructure skyward. Chunks of boiler plate whistled through the air like shrapnel. Jets of steam cooked men alive. Red-hot coals sizzled into the water or fell on the deck to start numerous fires. Hundreds of men were killed outright by the explosion or blown through the air into the swirling current. Seething masses of panic-stricken men grasped at anything to stay afloat and pulled each other under. The river was three miles wide at that point and in the pitch-black darkness it was almost impossible to see the shore. The turbulent stream, full of eddies and whirlpools, carried even the strongest swimmers under. The only hope for those in the water was to cling to a piece of the debris that littered the river.

Those not blasted into the stream by the explosion faced a worse fate. Many were trapped below deck and burned to death. Their screams filled the night air. Some jumped immediately into the river. Still others clung to the vessel until the fire reached them and they too dropped into the icy waters. The few lifeboats launched were soon swamped by the drowning hordes. Those still on the ship combed the wreckage for anything that would keep them afloat. The captain ripped off the cabin shutters and threw them to swimmers below. One soldier bayoneted the captive alligator and pushed himself overboard in the stout wooden cage. A passing boat rescued him miles downstream.

Meanwhile, the floating inferno that had once been the Sultana drifted out of control. When it lodged against a small island, some soldiers jumped ashore and secured the vessel with ropes. Another group of survivors fashioned a raft out of broken timbers and drifted loose just before the ship sunk with a great hiss and a cloud of steam.

Pvt. Chester Berry of the 20th Michigan Infantry had been awakened at the time of the explosion by a flying piece of wood that fractured his skull. The man next to him was scalded to death. Berry grabbed a few pieces of doorcasing and jumped into the river. An excellent swimmer, he stroked toward what he thought was a small island. When he made no headway he realized that he was trying to swim against the strong current. Exhausted, he floated with the help of his tiny raft of wood until he was able to grasp a tree top rising above the flooded river bank. Berry was eventually rescued by the gunboat Pocahontas that searched for survivors.

In 1892 Berry compiled a book containing the stories of as many fellow survivors as he could locate. Page after page of poignant testimony by Michigan, Indiana and Ohio men document miraculous escapes from the Sultana horror. A Pontiac man, J.E. Norton of the 5th Michigan Cavalry, awoke after the explosion to find himself pinned down by a heavy object. After struggling free, he assisted in raising timbers off other trapped soldiers and then floated down the river supported by a wooden box. Another panic-stricken soldier wrestled the box away and nearly drowned him, but Norton made it to safety, clinging to a bale of hay.

George F. Robinson of Charlotte was stunned by the explosion. The first thing he remembered was someone below him screaming "for God's sake, cut the deck, I am burning to death." His partner was laying across his legs, dead. Robinson survived by clinging to a dead mule. Others caught the tail of live mules, and a dozen men gripped one floundering horse.

Ogilvie E. Hamblin, a veteran from Jackson County, had had an arm amputated by Confederate surgeons. Nevertheless, he managed to float to shore where he clung to a treetop with his one arm until rescued. Many others who managed to make it to shore died of exposure or of the effects of their burns.

There was no official verification of the exact number of Sultana victims, but the best estimate places the death list at 1,700. Michigan's adjutant general, John Robertson, termed the Sultana explosion the greatest calamity of the Civil War. Strangely enough, newspapers of the time, preoccupied with the pursuit of Lincoln's assassins and the end of the war, devoted little space to the tragedy. Yet the sinking of the Sultana remains one of history's worst naval disasters.

When Pine Was King

Twenty-two million feet of timber at a banking ground on the Tittabawassee River in the 1880s.

The white pine had sprouted from a pine cone in the days of the Pilgrims. Six feet through at the base, it rose straight as an arrow, 100 feet tall. Its craggy branches stirred as a shiver ran through its trunk.

Far below its crown, antlike figures pulled a gleaming crosscut saw back and forth. Little streams of sawdust mounded up on each side. One of the men paused to pound wedges tighter into the gash cut by the saw, then returned to his rhythmic labor. With a sudden cry of "timber-r-r-r" one sawyer pulled his handle off the saw, the other yanked the blade through the cut and both ran for safety. The forest giant slowly began to topple, increasing in velocity until, with a crackling roar, it bounced on a pillow of snow.

Green gold they called the vast stands of white, red, and jack pine that blanketed Michigan's peninsulas north of the southern three tiers of counties. Woodworkers and builders preferred white pine, soft, easily shaped and durable. By the 1840s, as the last stand of white pine vanished before woodsmen's axes in Maine, the timber frontier shifted to Michigan.

During the period from 1860 to 1900 pine was king in Michigan and the harvesting, sawing and marketing of lumber dominated the state's economy. Some 160 billion board feet of Michigan timber flowed to eastern manufacturers, and to western prairie farmers, and it built Chicago twice. In 1890, the peak year, Michigan cut some 4¼ billion board feet of lumber.

Timber barons like Charles Hackley of Muskegon, Louis Sands of Manistee, and Perry Hannah of Traverse City made fortunes out of pine. Others mixed pine with politics to parley their success in lumbering into political careers. Michigan Governors Crapo, Alger, Jerome and Bliss started as lumbermen as did U.S. Senators Francis B. Stockbridge of Kalamazoo and Thomas W. Ferry of Grand Haven.

The big operators and thousands of less-successful entrepreneurs ruthlessly attacked the state's seemingly inexhaustible timber resources. They denuded virgin forests bought at $1.25 an acre or less into barren stretches of blow sand. Railroad companies received millions of acres of prime woods as a reward for extending their lines northward. Another infamous tactic was to "log a round forty" by buying forty acres in the middle of a stand and cutting the timber in all directions as far as could be seen. Reforestation or conservation of uncut trees was unheard of. Entire townships of cutover areas containing nothing but stumps and tinder-dry tops brought frequent forest fires. In 1871 and 1881 millions of acres of prime forests went up in flames.

Large-scale exploitation of Michigan's pine lands began when lumbermen in New England and New York learned of the enormous stands of white pine in the Saginaw River Basin. There, grew more than three million acres of the finest quality white pine, called cork pine because it floated high in the water like a cork. The Saginaw River Basin also contained 864 miles of rivers and streams suitable for floating logs to the saw mills. During the peak years of the 1880s, 110 sawmills lay along the Saginaw River from Saginaw through Bay City and on to Essexville. By 1897, when the timber ran out, almost 23 billion board feet of Saginaw lumber had been shipped by schooner or train to eastern markets.

On the western side of the lower peninsula, the Grand, Pere Marquette, Manistee, Betsie and Boardmen became famous lumber rivers. Major operations that rivaled the Saginaw Basin took place on the Muskegon River. As early as 1837, Augustus Penoyer sent a raft of lumber from his sawmill at Penoyer Creek down the Muskegon to Chicago. By the 1880s, 48 sawmills lined the banks of Muskegon Lake. When operations ceased in 1916, a total of 25 billion feet of timber had floated down the Muskegon River.

In the 1880s, many lumbermen began migrating to the Upper Peninsula. The Pine, Manistique, Sturgeon, Whitefish, Rapid, Escanaba, AuTrain and Tahquamenon Rivers were prime lumbering streams. The Menominee River, forming the boundary between Michigan and Wisconsin, carried the most timber. Dozens of sawmills dominated the economy of the twin cities of Marinette and Menominee, located on either side of the river. In 1891, the peak year, 642 million board feet of pine was cut on the Menominee alone.

The logging cycle began with the timber cruiser. Armed with a map and compass he would tramp the wilderness for weeks seeking prime stands of white pine located near a stream, then race to the nearest U.S. land office to register the find. In the fall, "road monkeys" cut a tote road into the site, "tote teamsters" brought in supplies and equipment and "wood butchers" threw together some primitive camp buildings. A full crew of "shanty boys" arrived by the first snowfall and spent the entire winter felling trees, "bucking" them into logs, skidding logs to the "cross-haul," and loading giant sleigh loads of logs that might weigh as much as 60,000 pounds. "Sprinklers" worked at night to create an icy trail, and horses shod with caulked shoes pulled sleighs to the banking grounds adjacent to a stream. The "chickadee's" humble but necessary task was to keep the logging trails free of horse manure.

In the spring, when the ice melted and the streams ran high, the shanty boys donned "corked" boots for the river drive. "River hogs" broke up the huge piles of logs at the rollway and rode logs downstream to the sorting booms at the booming grounds. Using pike poles and peavies they unsnarled log jams and retrieved beached logs. A floating kitchen and headquarters called a wanigan followed the drive. When the thousands of logs arrived at the booming grounds, sorters identified each company's logs by a distinctive mark similar to a cattle brand, that had been hammered into the end of the log.

The period when pine was king in Michigan brought wealth to timber barons, boom days for cities like Muskegon, Saginaw and Bay City and left a legacy of folk tales about one of America's most colorful professions, the lumberjack.

It Burned a Swath Across the State

Refugees from White Rock in Huron County escaped the fire that destroyed much of Michigan in 1871 by taking to Lake Huron's cold waters.

James Langworth did not get much sleep the night of October 8, 1871. As he lay in the bedroom of his farmhouse four miles south of the Saginaw County village of St. Charles, the wood smoke that had stung his eyes for a week nearly suffocated him. Langworth knew the forest fire was burning closer, but he relied on the half-mile-wide swamp that separated his farm from the woods to keep it away. He thought about the hundreds of rabbits, woodchucks, raccoons and squirrels that had milled around his barnyard that evening, so bewildered and blinded by the smoke they did not even fear man.

Shortly after midnight, Langworth felt the wind change direction and quicken. An hour later he could hear the roar of the fire and the crash of great trees toppling over. By 6 a.m., the high winds had fanned the fire around the swamp. Langworth gathered up a few personal belongings in a feather tick and opened his door. The smoke was so dense he could not see 10 feet away, and the air was "as hot as the atmosphere of an engine room."

Suddenly his barn and haystack exploded into flames. The gale-force wind sent thousands of sparks and firebrands into the air. Langworth dropped his bundle and ran for his life. Somehow he found the wagon road to the village and stumbled blindly down it. The fire raced close behind, showering him with burning debris. Then a sheet of flames swept across the road in front. The inferno surrounded him on all sides but one. He plunged into the woods leaping wildly over burning piles of leaves. It seemed as though the entire state of Michigan was on fire.

Much of it was. All summer long the northern United States had suffered one of the worst droughts on record. Farmers had watched their seedlings shrivel in the parched soil. The woods were dry and the vast stretches of cutover pine lands covered with brittle tree tops were like tinder. For months forest fires had raged throughout northern Wisconsin and Michigan. Billowing clouds of yellow smoke had produced memorable blood-red sunsets and caused the street lamps in Chicago to be lit an hour earlier than usual.

On October 8th, Mrs. O'Leary's cow or some other cause started a fire that leveled Chicago. That same evening a forest fire fed by hurricane-strength winds swept over the city of Peshtigo, Wisconsin and more than 1,000 victims died within hours. These disasters eclipsed Michigan's fiery holocaust in the national press, but the Michigan fires were more devastating in terms of property loss.

Fire ravished much of the Lake Michigan coast from St. Joseph to Manistee on October 8th. Most of the city of Holland, with the exception of the Hope College campus area, burned to the ground. A nasty rumor surfaced that a group of Hollanders refused to combat the brush fires that threatened the city from the southwest because it "would be wrong to do any work" on the Sabbath. Miraculously, only one person died in the conflagration, but the prosperous city was reduced to rubble in two hours.

One hundred miles to the north the rip-roaring lumbering town of Manistee faced a similar fate. Lumberjacks and townspeople battled scattered blazes in the city throughout the day. As with most lumbermill sites, flammable material was everywhere. Huge stacks of cordwood lined the docks, and extensive lumberyards with enormous mounds of sawdust dotted the village. The sidewalks were made of white pine and even the roads had been paved with sawdust. That evening a gale force wind blew in an irresistible fire storm from the south that engulfed the city in flames. Over 1,000 people wandered homeless through the ruins the next morning.

The forest fires burned a swath of destruction straight across the state to Lake Huron. Lansing escaped destruction due largely to the efforts of Agricultural College students who turned out en masse to battle the flames. Much of the forests of Midland and Gratiot Counties were reduced to smouldering stumps. The Saginaw River Valley fared little better. The fire that had sent Langworth fleeing into the woods raged from St. Charles to Birch Run. Langworth stumbled into the outskirts of St. Charles, his face blistered and clothing burned full of holes, to encounter the entire village mobilized to protect their holdings.

Michigan's thumb area was particularly hard hit. The lakeshore settlements of Grindstone City, Huron City, Port Hope, and White Rock were all but wiped out. Most of Huron, Tuscola and Sanilac Counties went up in flames.

At Forestville John Kent and his wife left their two children in their dwelling as they beat back brush fires. Unknown to them, another fire from the rear reached the house. By the time they heard the children's screams, the smoke had become so dense they could not find their way back. Kent and his wife narrowly escaped by running to the lake, but as he told a Port Huron reporter, "It was awful, sir, to hear that screaming from those burning children, and it was dreadful to go away and leave them roasting there."

Undoubtedly, many other backwoods families perished and were never accounted for. But the actual loss of life in Michigan was remarkably small. Many miraculous escapes were recorded. Entire families survived by lowering themselves into wells. Others took to Lake Huron in boats and, despite the rough waters, were later rescued.

One small vessel containing nine children from Rock Falls, a Huron County ghost town, floated for three days all the way across Lake Huron to Canada. All but one child survived the ordeal.

The inhabitants of White Rock fought the blaze all day

Sunday, but when the fierce gale fanned the fire out of control they ran for the lake. For eight hours they huddled in the ice cold surf, adults taking turns holding the children. When the fire died down they warmed themselves by the embers of their village until they were rescued by a ship.

Michigan's death toll numbered at least 10 and probably many more. The fire raged across an estimated 2½ million acres of land and destroyed at least 4 billion feet of prime timber.

A Pulpit in the Pines

FLORENCE COTTAGES

BAY VIEW

Rooms to Rent

In a beautiful and central location. In same block with Post Office, Hotel and Restaurant and convenient to Railroad Depot and Ferry Landing.

Several Cottages for Rent Furnished complete for Housekeeping

Sleeping Rooms, $3.50 to $7.00 per week.

Also Rooms for Light Houskeeping.
BATH ROOMS.

Six well located cottages for rent or sale
Terms reasonable.

MRS. KATE LEWIS, - Park Ave., Bay View, Mich.

A 1913 advertisement promoted one of the stately cottages built at Bay View to accommodate visitors to the Methodist campground.

The rustic pulpit fashioned from an uprooted birch stood in the center of a northern Michigan forest clearing. Towering Rev. Seth Reed, whom local Indians had named "Straight-up-Through-the-Sky," boomed out a benediction. His Methodist brethren, seated on rough plank boards before him, bowed their heads in prayer.

The light from flickering torches highlighted an occasional standing Indian whose shining dark eyes watched the white man's camp meeting. White canvas tents crowded the periphery of the clearing. Beyond stretched a primeval forest of beech, maple, hemlock, birch, poplar and pine. During lulls in the preacher's exhortations and the weeping of penitents could be heard the distant roar of waves sweeping the sandy shore of Little Traverse Bay.

It was August 1876 and some 500 Methodists from across the state had gathered at a wilderness tract immediately northeast of Petoskey to found what the Rev. Reed named the Bay View Camp Ground Association. Its purpose was to provide a natural site "to hold camp meetings, and moral and religious services thereon for moral and religious purposes, and for scientific and intellectual culture".

Methodist camp meetings, where itinerant preachers shouted sinners into hysterical frenzy, had been an important part of American frontier culture since the 1790s. Such revivals also served as important social gatherings where isolated settlers could learn the latest gossip and young couples might do a little "sparking." In 1875 Dr. John Vincent founded the Chautauqua Assembly on a lake in western New York as a permanent summer camp meeting and training school for Methodist Sunday School teachers. Michigan Methodist leaders determined to develop a similiar facility.

The Rev. Joseph McCarty, pastor of the Methodist Church in Jackson, campaigned for a northern

Michigan campground where cool westerly breezes and invigorating northern air would make an ideal vacation spot within easy reach of Chicago. Mr. and Mrs. S.O. Knapp, two of McCarty's parishioners, had passed the previous summer in Petoskey in search of a cure for Mrs. Knapp's respiratory problems. They spent much of their leisure time rambling along the shoreline northeast of the town. There they discovered a wonderland of wooded terraaces, some 40 natural springs and breathtaking views of the bay.

When the Knapp's told their pastor of their discovery, he began negotiations with the Grand Rapids and Indiana Railroad. By emphasizing the passenger business such a campground might bring, McCarty convinced the railroad to provide free land. In September 1875, the Michigan Annual Conference of the Methodist Church appointed a committee to select the site.

Citizens of other northern locales boosted their respective attractions with offers of free land and financial allurements. The GR&I Railroad conveyed the committee on a special excursion train to Petoskey. At Traverse City, on the return trip, a crowd of citizens met the committee at the depot for a carriage tour of their environs. The Flint and Pere Marquette Railroad provided a similar junket to Ludington. Cheboygan, Otsego Lake and Cadillac also offered land for the meeting ground. But after four months of travel and research the committee decided on Petoskey.

A number of problems developed. The GR&I Railroad did not want to pay for extending its line from Petoskey to Bay View. Petoskey citizens had little available cash, but they pledged $3,400 worth of their labor. During the summer of 1876, local workmen constructed tracks made of wooden rails covered with strap iron, not strong enough to support a locomotive. A Petoskey citizen bought a defunct horse-drawn street car in Kalamazoo.

Passengers coasted downhill from Petoskey to the camp ground, and the car was pulled back by a horse.

Another obstacle lay in the fact that the railroad did not actually own all the Bay View property. A GR&I Railroad land agent and H.O. Rose, a Petoskey entrepreneur, spent the winter of 1875 traveling by pony and cutter among the Indians scattered from Sault Ste. Marie to Traverse City buying the shoreland. Finally on May 22, 1876, the GR&I conveyed title to 326 acres of land at Bay View to the Camp Ground Association.

Meanwhile, a delegation had traveled to Bay View to lay out the campground. Stumbling through the "shintangle" blanketing the forest floor, they laid out a serpentine plat that followed the lay of the land. Organizational meetings held by Methodist Congregations in Jackson, Ann Arbor, Kalamazoo, Detroit and Grand Rapids promoted the venture. Initially, members received a 15-year lease on a lot for $10. Before anyone could become a member of the association, lease a lot or build a cottage, however, their spiritual and moral character had to be approved by the association.

Many of the original members camped in tents throughout the summers. Eventually, however, most erected fashionable Queen Anne-style cottages intricately decorated with gingerbread trim. For many years, the campground retained its austere religious environment. The highlight of each summer was a massive camp meeting called "Big Sunday" which drew thousands of visitors.

Despite the allure of Little Traverse Bay, few of the Bay View pioneers braved swimming. Their reluctance came not so much from moral grounds as from the current medical philosophy. A Dr. Wood, for example, assured a young woman camper in 1878 that "Lake Michigan is not fit for anyone to bathe in."

Gradually Bay View lost most of its religious

emphasis. By the 1890s, it had become more of a cultural experience, similar to the tent Chautauqua concept. Nationally famous lecturers including William Jennings Bryan, Helen Keller, Frances E. Willard and Booker T. Washington spoke at Bay View. The Bay View Reading Circle, a home extension course that led to an honorary degree, began in 1893. The organization published text-books and the *Bay View Magazine*, and its membership eventually reached 25,000. A summer college affiliated with Albion College operated at Bay View until 1969. In 1972 the entire Bay View Camp Ground was placed on the National Register of Historic Sites.

Grand Rapids: The Furniture City

FUR AND BUSINESS DIRECTORY. FUR 1225

CAPITAL, $300,000.

PHOENIX FURNITURE CO.

MANUFACTURERS OF

West Side, on Fulton, Summer and Winter Streets,

GRAND RAPIDS, MICH.

NEW YORK WAREROOMS, - 175 and 177 CANAL STREET.

An 1880 advertisement for one of Grand Rapids' largest furniture firms.

It must have been the biggest, most ornate bed in the world, a pallet fit for a king. A man standing on his tiptoes on another's shoulders could not touch the top of the backboard. Constructed of slabs of elaborately carved Michigan black walnut inlaid with French burl, Grand Rapids-based Nelson, Matter and Company's unique bed featured numerous niches for statuettes. Columbia flanked by Gutenburg and Columbus stood within the footboard, and classic bronzes with uplifted arms posed atop each bedpost. Ebony pillars supported a backboard resembling a medieval altar, the center occupied by a large statue of George Washington. A huge wooden eagle with widespread wings surmounted the Victorian masterpiece.

Made specially for showing at the Philadelphia Centennial Exposition of 1876, Nelson, Matter and Company's "Centennial Bedstead" stole the show. Thousands of furniture fanciers from across the country gazed in awe at the huge bedstead and matching dressing case and bureau. The suite carried a price tag of $10,000, at a time when factory workers earned an average $1 for a 10-hour work day, and a square mile of government land sold for $800.

Nelson, Matter and Company's exhibit and other less pretentious bedroom suites displayed by Berkey and Gay and The Phoenix Furniture Company, also of Grand Rapids, won medals at the exposition. They also first attracted widespread interest in Grand Rapids' furniture. Following the exposition, the three companies leased showrooms in New York City. By 1878, as furniture buyers began flocking to local factories, Grand Rapids was well on its way to becoming "Furniture City" to the nation.

A variety of factors won Grand Rapids its new title. Situated amidst vast tracts of virgin forests, white pine to the north and black walnut, cherry, white ash, basswood, hard maple, red oak, hickory and other desirable hardwoods to the south, Grand Rapids manufacturers enjoyed abundant supplies of cheap furniture-grade lumber. Transportation routes offered access to a wide market. In the early days, steamers transported cargo to Grand Haven for shipment to Chicago, Detroit, Buffalo, etc. In 1858, the Detroit and Milwaukee railroad reached Grand Rapids to offer cheap reliable year-round transportation. Also by 1856, locally produced woodworking machinery and steam engines began surplanting the original waterpowered factories. Perhaps the most important asset was the presence of skilled entrepreneurs who would parley these natural advantages into furniture empires.

William Haldane, the city's pioneer furniture maker, emigrated from New York state via Ohio. He set up a furniture shop in his home at the southwest corner of Pearl Street and Ottawa Avenue. Using a treadle-powered lathe and hand tools, Hanldane produced durable chairs, beds and tables. Typical of early furniture makers, he also turned out a line of coffins. Other early woodworkers including Archibald Salmon, Samuel F. Butcher, Abram Snively, and David Wooster, largely emigrants from New England and New York, an area known for a tradition of fine furniture craftsmanship, established small factories in the 1830s and 1840s.

Prior to the 1850s, most Grand Rapids manufacturers catered predominantly to the local market. A major problem with some wares, however, stemmed from the use of green or unseasoned lumber. Furniture constructed of uncured stock would later warp, shrink and fall apart. Local pioneers remembered buying bureaus and sets of chairs that they later returned to the maker in gunnysacks.

By the 1850s, facilities for curing wood and manufacturing techniques had improved to allow ventures into more distant markets. E.M. Ball, a schoolteacher from New Hampshire, went into partnership with William Powers in 1849. The firm of Powers and Ball sought trade outside Grand Rapids. Following a trip "over the lakes" in 1851, Powers secured an order for 10,000 chairs to be delivered to Chicago. Typical prices charged by Powers and Ball were $2.50 for a "sett" of chairs, $2 for a bedstead, $4 for a table and 75 cents for a highchair.

C.C. Comstock, who had taken over the firm ot Winchester Brothers following its bankruptcy during the financial "panic of 1857", reorganized it as Comstock, Nelson and Co. in 1863. He actively promoted furniture sales in distant cities. During the 1870s, when Comstock disposed of his interests, the firm became Nelson, Matter and Co. By 1890 employment reached 450, and the firm had won the reputation as "the largest and best known manufacturer of its day."

Traditionally, furniture salesmen used miniature models to illustrate the various styles they carried. In 1862, Elias Matter began substituting photographs for miniature samples. His success spurred general adaptation to photographic displays. Other early salesmen filled railroad cars with samples and peddled their products along side railings across the nation. Englishman George Widdicomb arrived in 1856 to found a furniture dynasty. His four sons later organized the William Widdicomb Company and the John Widdicomb Company. In 1877, the William Widdicomb Company issued the first local furniture catalog illustrated by woodcuts.

Other famous 19th century Grand Rapids furniture firms included The Grand Rapids Chair Co., incorporated in 1872, The Luce Furniture Co., a descendant of the John Bradfield Co. founded in 1874, the Sligh Furniture Co., which became one of the city's largest, and the American Seating Company. Stow and

Davis trace their heritage to 1880.

During the 1880s and 1890s, some 85 furniture manufacturers went into production in Grand Rapids. Grand Rapids furniture gained additional fame through extensive exhibits at the World's Exposition at New Orleans in 1884 and the Columbian Exposition in 1893. By 1928, when the city celebrated its 100th semi-annual furniture exposition, 365 different manufacturers, including companies from New York, Chicago, Milwaukee, St. Louis and many Michigan cities, capitalized on the Furniture City's good name to fill more than 2,400,000 square feet with displays.

South Haven's Native Naturalist

Liberty Hyde Bailey, world renowned horticulturist from South Haven.

Maria Bailey peered into her oven, trying to adjust her eyes to the darkness. Suddenly she let out a shriek and slammed the oven door. "Snakes! Snakes," she screamed, "Liberty Hyde Bailey come here!"

A frail, 10-year-old boy, blue eyes wide with excitement, appeared. "They're only milk snakes. I put the eggs in the oven to hatch," he said. "I'm studying them."

The young naturalist's father had recently cleaned out a menagerie of snakes, lizards, frogs and other speciments Bailey had secreted in the farm's tool shed. He thought his kindly stepmother might be more tolerant of his pursuits, but the baby milk snakes soon received the same treatment.

Bailey's father, a stern Vermonter of Puritan heritage, held little shift for idle play, even for a child. But eventually young Bailey's intense love of nature won him over. He tolerated his investigations so long as they did not impinge on chores, school work or the Sabbath - and were conducted outdoors. This childhood enthusiasm for observing nature would blossom into a lifelong passion for discovery, and Liberty Hyde Bailey would win distinction as one of America's leading botanists and horticulturalists.

Bailey's father had immigrated to Michgian in 1842, finding work on the Michigan Central Railroad that was pushing its way across the state. He married Sarah Harrison in Kalamazoo in 1845, and they settled on a 40-acre homestead in Arlington Township, Van Buren County. A decade later, Bailey sold his farm and bought another located about a mile southeast of the frontier settlement at the mouth of the Black River, called South Haven. Bailey constructed a sturdy frame house in the familiar Greek Revival style of architecture in 1858 and it was there that in March of that year his third-born son and namesake came into the world.

A scenario all too common on the Michigan frontier ensued. Bailey's oldest son, Dana, died of scarlet fever in 1861, and the following year, the family watched helplessly as their mother succumbed to diphtheria. Young Liberty, a sensitive child of four, recalled nearly 90 years later, "I remember standing by the bed and seeing her pass into the silence".

The Bailey family channeled its bereavement into the continuous round of hard work demanded by Michigan farm life. Lacking a baby-sitter, young Liberty was left to his own devices. He wandered through his father's orchard, explored the mysteries of puddles alive with tadpoles, climbed sand dunes, listened to bird sounds, felt the texture of moss, lost himself in the ethereal world of clouds and breathed deeply the fecund fragrance of the swamp. Plants in particular fascinated him, and his father taught him how to take care of his mother's flower garden.

Soon Bailey entered school, and during the daily mile-long walk to the South Haven schoolhouse his imagination and curiosity about nature were further stimulated. He was fortunate in school to have a good teacher who encouraged and taught him not only to look but also to discriminate and remember what he saw. A Potawatomi Indian village located on a corner of his father's land offered additional learning experiences. Bailey's Indian friends taught him to hunt and trap as well as their philosophy about nature.

When Bailey first learned to read, the family library consisted only of the Bible, Josephus and The Pilgrim's Progress. When he had worked his way through those, each year his father bought him a new book about African explorations or life in the American War. In the early 1870s, a lending library was established in a back room of one of South Haven's stores. There Bailey encountered a volume that proved a milestone in his intellectual development. It was a copy of Darwin's *On the Origin of Species by Natural Selection.*

But in the 1870s, the very word evolution was considered indecent by many "God-fearing" folks. Bailey presented the volume to his father and asked permission to read it. He returned the book to his son a few days later saying, "I can't understand much of this, but I think the man is honest and means to tell the truth. You may read it." The incomprehensible Latin words scattered throughout the text spurred young Bailey to study that language.

Bailey's father, an expert fruit grower, had taught his son the art of grafting at the age of ten. By the time he was fourteen, he had earned a local reputation as a skilled grafter in his own right. About that time he read his first paper, "On the Grafting of Fruit Trees", before the South Haven Pomological Society. In 1873, his second paper, an impassioned plea for the protection of birds, was printed in the annual report of the State Pomological Society.

Four years later, Bailey had decided to attend the Michigan Agricultural College at East Lansing. The entire college enrollment in 1877 was 150 students, but the faculty was well qualified. In particular, William Beal, professor of botany and horticulture, became Bailey's mentor. Following graduation in 1882, Beal recommended Bailey for a position under world-famous botanist Asa Gray at Harvard University. In 1885, Bailey returned to his alma mater to fill the newly created chair of horticulture and landscape gardening.

Inadequate funding at M.A.C. prohibited the degree of experimentation Bailey craved. Consequently, in 1888 he leaped at the opportunity to join the faculty at amply endowed Cornell University. His association with Cornell continued until his retirement as dean in 1913. Over that 25-year span, through his prestige and drive, he converted a small agricultural college into a world-famous institution.

Bailey was a gifted teacher, administrator and scientist, but his writings stand as his major accomplishments. He was able to bridge the gap between botany, the scientific study of plants, and its practical application in horticulture. Beginning with a slim volume titled *Talks Afield* in 1886, Bailey was to write or edit nearly 50 volumes on subjects ranging from gourds to palm trees.

Following his so-called retirement from academic work, Bailey continued to study, travel and write about the nature he loved. His last book, *The Garden of Bellflowers*, was published in 1953. Bailey died at the age of 97 the following year. South Haven preserves the birthplace of its most honored native son as an historical museum.

The Pigeons Came to Petoskey

Ornithological artist Louis Agassiz Fuertes painted the last of a dying species in 1906.

Pigeon feathers carpeted the rutted road that wound through the woods. The worst of the sloughs had been filled in with wagonloads of pigeon wings. Long before the stream of hunters reached the nesting grounds, the cacophony of bird voices and the roar of beating wings drowned out all other sounds. It was the spring of 1878, and a record wild pigeon roost 40 miles long by three to 10 miles wide had been discovered just north of Petoskey.

Wild pigeons, or passenger pigeons, resembled mourning doves but were twice as large and had a beautiful plumage. Males were slate blue with brownish-red breasts and brilliant orange eyes, and hens were somewhat duller in appearance and slightly smaller. The huge flights of pigeons that migrated in search of food had amazed generations of frontiersmen.

Ornithologist John James Audubon had witnessed a flight in 1813 that darkened the sky like an eclipse for three days on end. The birds flew approximately 60 miles per hour, and Audubon had computed that an average-sized flock which took three hours to pass overhead contained more than one billion pigeons.

The pigeons nested in such huge numbers that they destroyed entire forests by breaking down trees under their combined weight. They fed on beechnuts, acorns, wild berries and insects. When they moved on, miles of land lay bare except for a blanket of droppings several inches deep. Following an impressive mating ritual, pairs of pigeons fashioned flimsy nests which held one or two eggs. Parents pushed fledglings out of the nest in about one month and bred again as many as four times a year.

News of pigeon roosts spread quickly through frontier communities as men, women and children dropped everything else to harvest the seemingly inexhaustible supply of birds. But by the last third of the 19th century, passenger pigeons had grown scarce in the eastern states. Michigan, however, remained a favored nesting ground. Alternate years corresponding to the cycles of nut-bearing trees drew enormous flocks.

Prior to the Civil War, pigeon roosts were plentiful throughout the southern tiers of counties, but as the forests disappeared the flocks shifted farther north. A major nesting occurred near Vassar, Tuscola County in 1866 and eight years later near Shelby, Oceana County. Then in 1878, a great flight from the south and another from across Lake Michigan converged near Petoskey to create the state's largest recorded roost.

Local families hastened to cash in on this avian windfall by filling up larders depleted by the severe winter. Meanwhile, an itinerant army of professional "pigeoners" estimated at 2,000 strong descended from all directions on the frontier community.

Some hunters used shotguns, bringing as many as two dozen birds down with one blast. Local Indians preferred long poles and blunt arrows with which they knocked the tasty "butterball" squabs out of their nest. Professional pigeoners, however, favored netting their prey.

After clearing the ground of underbrush, pigeoners baited a plot with salt, which the birds craved. On each side of the salt bed a net about six feet wide by 20 to 30 feet long was secured to powerful spring poles. The flutterings of a blinded bird known as a "stool pigeon" fastened to a device that was raised up and down lured pigeons to the trap. The operator watched in concealment until the seasoned bed was covered with pigeons then yanked a rope that sprung the clap net. A good catch might yield as many as 1,300 birds enmeshed in one net. Pigeoners deftly nipped the necks of the struggling birds with blacksmith's pincers, threw their bodies in a pile and reset the trap. Some professionals caught 5,000 birds per day using one net.

Local teamsters made good money hauling wagons heaped with deap pigeons to Petoskey. There, packers salted the birds in barrels which were shipped by rail or steamer to Chicago and other urban markets. At the nesting area, dead birds were worth 35 to 40 cents a dozen, squabs a penny apiece and live birds 40 to 60 cents a dozen. Live birds were in great demand by eastern sporting clubs for trapshooting. One pigeoner at Petoskey was reported to have earned $60,000 over a number of seasons.

Michigan game laws which prohibited hunting within five miles of the roost or netting within two miles of nesting grounds were unenforced and routinely violated. Saginaw and Bay City game protection clubs attempted to halt the illegal activity. Professor H.B. Roney of East Saginaw traveled to Petoskey with club representatives and recorded the wanton slaughter. With the aid of the local sheriff, Roney routed over 400 Indians out of the nesting one day. Despite angry pigeoners who threatened to "buckshot" him, he swore out warrants against netters operating near the rookery.

During the brief period Roney and his party were at Petoskey, they managed to dramatically reduce the number of pigeons shipped. But because of lack of funds they soon departed, and the "pigeon war" continued unchecked.

For twenty weeks beginning on March 22, rail shipments from Petoskey averaged 12,500 dead birds daily. Steamers from Petoskey, Cheboygan and Cross Village conveyed many more. Roney estimated that, including the dead and wounded not secured and the many squabs that died in the nest after their parents were trapped, a grand total of one billion pigeons had been "sacrificed to mammon during the nesting of 1878."

Meanwhile, on the western Great Plains as hide hunters mopped up the last of the great bison herds a new enterprise prospered - the sale of buffalo bones for fertilizer.

The 1878 nesting at Petoskey was the last in Michigan large enough for commercial exploitation. Smaller nestings were reported into the 1890s, but by the turn of the century everyone realized the wild pigeons had all but disappeared. On September 1, 1914, the last known passenger pigeon on earth died at the Cincinnati Zoological Gardens.

Turkey Feathers Meant Big Business

The first featherbone factory (left) revolutionized the corset industry.

The distinguished clubwoman arose amidst applause to accept the award. A buxom matron fond of ladyfingers and bonbons, she, nevertheless, displayed a perfect hourglass figure. All went well until she bent to retrieve a dropped leaf of notes. Then it happened. There was a crackling noise like small bones being broken and a ripping of silken material. The whalebone stays in her corset had snapped. Panic-stricken, she straightened up and tried mightily to suck it in. It was no use - for this Victorian damsel, the sands in the hourglass had run out.

Real-life versions of this scenario happened all too frequently in the days when American female pulchritude relied heavily on tightly laced corsets. Despite stern admonitions by doctors, most women preferred to mortify their internal organs rather than defy fashion's dictates. The instruments of torture, corsets, were stiffened by stays of whalebone (actually baleen, a horny substance with which certain types of whales sieve their diet of plankton from ocean waters). Therein lay the problem. As whalebone aged, it lost its elasticity and was prone to break at the most inopportune times. What's more, on hot summer days it had the tendency to give off a slightly fishy odor. Also, as harpooners hunted whales to near extinction, baleen became increasingly more expensive.

Edward K. Warren, who operated a general store in the Berrien County hamlet of Three Oaks, carried whalebone among his 1000 and one items of stock. When a customer complained that Warren's whalebone was brittle and useless and blamed him for it, he began to mull over the problem. What this country needed, decided the young entrepreneur, was a good substitute for whalebone.

The genesis of the solution came when Warren visited a feather duster factory in Chicago. There he saw piles of turkey feathers being burned. They were pointer quills, lacking plumage on one side, hence not suitable for dusters. The idea of something like turkey feathers having no use bothered Warren. He thought about it for more than a year before he got a brainstorm. Why not utilize quills, which had a similar elastic property, as a substitute for whalebone?

By the next day he had coined the name for his new discovery - "featherbone." That was the easy part. It took Warren several frustrating years of tinkering before he figured out how to actually manufacture a satisfactory featherbone. George R. Holden, a machinist from Michigan City, Indiana, designed the special equipment necessary. In 1883, Warren secured his first patent for featherbone.

Warren's ingenious process stripped the feathers of their plumage, split the quills in half, removed the pith and sliced the quills into fiber. This material fed into a machine emerged as a cord tightly wound with thread. Four cords sewed together produced a strong elastic flat tape - featherbone - ideal for sewing directly to corsets.

In June 1883, the Warren Featherbone Company was organized with a capital stock of $100,000. By September, workmen had laid the foundation for a small factory building on North Elm Street in Three Oaks. Most local observers thought the idea of making featherbone preposterous. W.K. Sawyer, editor of the Three Oaks Sun, quipped "No doubt quills will be fed in at one end and ready-made corsets be discharged from the other." Despite such sarcasm, production of featherbone began on November 15, 1883.

Within a month, the little plant was operating at full capacity. A work force consisting of one foreman, two boys and six girls produced 2,000 yards of featherbone daily. Orders poured in from all over the country. The factory ran out of feathers in January and temporarily closed down. By May 1884, Warren was desperately advertising in neighboring towns for additional workers. Townspeople gazed in awe as long lines of boxcars loaded with turkey quills and passenger cars carrying rosy-cheeked misses, who had left the farm for the featherbone factory, lumbered into Three Oaks.

In September, a night shift went into operation. By Christmas time, 20 tons of turkey feathers had been crammed into a large new warehouse, and every spare room in Three Oaks was crowded with new Featherbone employees.

In February 1885, Warren diversified into production of buggy whips containing a filler of featherbone. The featherbone whip sold well. So well, that Charles H. Clark, a prominent whip maker from Rochester, New York, announced plans to build a new factory to manufacture Warren's whips. Grand Rapids, Niles, Saginaw, St. Joseph and other Michigan cities vied for the new factory.

Editor Sawyer, now an enthusiastic featherbone boomer, led Three Oaks citizens in their bid to retain the industry. Three Oaks won out when local farmers and villagers subscribed $10,000 in stock in the company. A new three-story Featherbone Whip factory went into production on September 15, 1885. By January of the following year, salesmen canvassed the country with a line of 150 different featherbone whips.

Continued prosperity spurred the development of branch factories in Middleville, Michigan, Porter, Indiana and St. Thomas, Canada. By the turn of the century, the Warren Featherbone Company had become such a dominant force in Three Oaks that it published the only paper, *The Three Oaks Acorn*. Warren, the son of a Congregational minister, also saw to it that his personal ethics were followed locally. In 1899, Warren offered to pay the village treasurer the $250 saloon license fees then being received. From that day on, Warren paid $250 each year and Three Oaks went dry.

In 1901, Warren experimented with a trade

publication called the *Featherbone Magazinette.* It carried testimonials by famous people such as actress Sarah Bernhardt who wrote in her less than perfect English, "I have always Warren's Featherbone used in my costumes, for I believe it to be the best dress boning material in existence."

In 1891, one of Warren's employees started a related venture, the Featherbone Corset Company. James H. Hatfield relocated the factory to Kalamazoo and a few years later renamed his growing enterprise the Kalamazoo Corset Company. By the turn of the century it had become the largest corset factory in the world, employing over 700 women.

The flapper era of the 1920s, which favored the boyish look in women's fashions, delivered a death blow to the corset industry. The Warren Featherbone Company diversified into other dressmaker supplies and survived in a diminished capacity through the Depression era.

The man who had established a dynasty based on turkey feathers, died in 1919. His name survives in Warren Dunes State Park on the shores of Lake Michigan.

A Sinister Horde Hailed From Seney

Carl Guldberg's painting of the 1891 Dunn- Harcourt fight.

His nose had been bitten off in a drunken brawl, and his face sported a good case of "logger's smallpox" caused by multiple stompings with caulked boots. P.K. Small was one of the toughest, meanest, ugliest lumberjacks in the state, and when he was not wrestling white pine in the woods he was on a drunk, in a fight or usually both. He stepped into the Saginaw train depot one day and roared "I want a ticket to Hell." The agent calmly handed him a ticket to Seney.

Seney, located about halfway between Newberry and Munising in the Upper Peninsula, sprang into being in 1882 when the Alger, Smith Company began logging the vast stands of white pine that blanketed the vicinity. A dozen or so other logging outfits soon followed suit, and most set up their headquarters in Seney. Within a few years, Seney boasted a population of 3,000, including a substantial number of outlaws, con men, prostitutes and other dregs of society that had drifted to this Sodom of the North. So many "lost men" lived there that during the 1880s and 1890s the Detroit Post Office routinely forwarded mail from its dead-letter file to Seney.

During its heyday, each spring a horde of wild lumberjacks who had been pent up in the surrounding woods all winter doubled Seney's population. They came looking for a good time, and the town's 21 saloons, four or five blind pigs and five bordellos stood ready to oblige them. Because the Fox River periodically flooded the site, all the buildings stood on stilts. Even the wooden sidewalks rose a foot or two above the ground.

When Seney's notoriety drifted eastward, a delegation of newspaper reporters, including one of the few women journalists of the time, arrived to investigate. The woman reporter found the widespread gambling, brawling, drunkenness and prostitution mild compared to the "Ram's Pasture." Strangers, she wrote, were being "shanghaied" on the frontier, forced to work in the woods and herded each night into a stockaded Ram's Pasture. Any who attempted escape were tracked down by fierce mastiffs. Her expose made headlines across the country.

This lawlessness on the Michigan frontier so shocked the nation that a congressional committee was organized to investigate. But Wall Street lumbermen and Michigan politicians mollified the officials by explaining that local pranksters had duped the reporter with a wild hoax. The Ram's Pasture was merely an overcrowded hotel where men slept on the floor in shifts, and the mastiffs were raised by a local bartender for the general market. Despite this logical explanation, a good share of the public continued to believe tales of slavery in Seney.

Periodically, other sensational stories from Seney enlivened headlines. There was the widely reported Dunn-Harcourt feud, for example. Dan Dunn, a notorious desperado, had fled a bench warrant at Roscommon to Seney, where he set up a saloon and bawdy house. When the old lumberjack who Dunn had paid to torch his bar in Roscommon for an insurance scam followed him to Seney, he murdered him and hid his body. The same thing happened to a creditor from Roscommon who tried to collect. Some of the six Harcourt brothers operated a tavern at Roscommon. A grudge had developed between them and Dunn. The feud intensified when the Harcourts also moved to Seney and opened a saloon across the street from Dunn's.

On June 25, 1891, 20-year-old Steve Harcourt entered Dunn's, walked up to the 40-foot-long bar and ordered a round for the house. Instead, Dunn smashed a bottle over Harcourt's head, reached under the bar for a gun and shot him through the jaw. Harcourt pulled a pistol out of his pocket but only succeeded in plugging a hole in a portrait of pugilist John L. Sullivan that hung behind the bar. Dunn shot Harcourt again, in the side. Harcourt died two or three days later. Dunn was arrested for manslaughter but succeeded in getting the charge dropped through bribery and political connections.

The five remaining Harcourts drew straws over who would avenge their brother, and Jim got the short straw. Dunn fled for Canada, but Harcourt caught up with him at a saloon in Trout Lake. In the ensuing shoot-out, Harcourt pumped four bullets into Dunn's body before he hit the floor. Convicted of murder, Harcourt was pardoned by the governor after three years, largely due to a widely circulated petition that claimed he had rendered a service to the state by eliminating the "Northern Peninsula Terror."

Most Seney shenanigans turned out less fatal than the Dunn-Harcourt feud, but a coterie of colorful characters insured there was never a dull moment. Old P.K. Small retired from lumbering into a full-time life in the barrooms. He earned the title "Snag Jaw" through his practice of biting the heads off of live snakes, toads and frogs for a free drink. Once when a pet crow landed on his shoulder, he turned around and bit its head off too. Many a greenhorn who arrived at the Seney depot experienced another of P.K.'s favorite tricks. He would collect what he called a "loose offering" by sneaking up behind the stranger, grabbing him around the middle, turning him upside down and shaking the change out of his pockets.

Another local character, "Old Light Heart," loved to eat raw liver. After a drunken jag, he'd curl up in two old sugar barrels laid end to end. One cold night he lost his toes to frostbite. Thereafter, "Pump Handle Joe" and his buddy, "Frying Pan Mag", amused themselves by nailing the old drunk's shoes to the floor and watching him pitch forward when he tried to stand.

"Silver Jack" Driscoll, a legendary brawler who approached Paul Bunyan in fame, called Seney home in the 1880s. At one time he served as a bartender and bouncer for Dunn. Leon Czolgosz was probably the most notorious of the sinister horde who hailed from Seney. When he lost his job as a railroad section hand he went to Cleveland, got fired up by one of anarchist Emma Goldman's speeches and assassinated President William McKinley in Buffalo in 1901.

By the mid 1890s, only stumps remained of the majestic white pine forest in the Seney vicinity. The lumbering companies moved their headquarters to Grand Marais and elsewhere, and without the lumberjack's trade the town dried up. Today, the place once known as the toughest town in Michigan is a tiny crossroad hamlet. A restaurant operated by Mennonite folk serves one of the best pasties available in the U.P. They don't even sell cigarettes in an adjoining general store. But across the street at the Seney Bar, it's not hard to imagine that a stranger from "down below" might still get the change shaken out of his pockets.

The P.T. Barnum of Haberdashery

Little Jake Seligman, Saginaw's most flamboyant haberdasher.

The statue of a broad-shouldered hero, twelve feet tall, stood atop the tower of the "flatiron" building at the triangular point where Genesee and Lapeer Streets meet in downtown Saginaw. Below the majestic copper monument the four faces of a huge clock bore the inscription "Little Jake's Time." For half a century, the clock tower and its imposing likeness of Little Jake Seligman reminded Saginaw residents of the feats of one of Michigan's most flamboyant merchants.

Born of humble Jewish parents in Darnstadt. Germany, Jacob Seligman immigrated to New York City in 1859 at the age of 16. Following a year's apprenticeship under a New York tailor, Seligman moved to Pontiac, Michigan with Louis Goodman, another tailor who had befriended him. In Pontiac he worked for Goodman, saving every penny he could out of his $4 per week salary.

Three years later, Seligman had amassed $100, enough, he thought, to begin his own career as a clothing merchant. He struck an agreement with the Heavenrich Brothers of Detroit whereby they furnished the merchandise and he split the net profits with them. In January 1863, Seligman opened for business on Saginaw Street in Pontiac.

Capitalizing on his most conspicuous trait, his size, or lack of it, the 4-foot-11-inch haberdasher named his firm "Little Jake's". Soon, all the Pontiac newspapers as well as most of the fences, trees and barns in the region carried Little Jake's innovative advertising. In an age when colorful promotion was largely the domain of circuses and patent medicine hucksters Little Jake outdid even them. He not only informed the public in large letters that his stock was the best and his prices the cheapest, but he infuriated competitors by ridiculing them by name. A master of hyperbole, Little Jake trumpeted that his fledging business was "the largest retail clothier in Michigan".

Perhaps because of his aggressive advertising, within a few years Little Jake was well on the road of becoming just that. His favorite stunt was to hire a brass band to parade through the streets of Pontiac until it stopped in front of his store for a concert. Whereupon Little Jake appeared at an upstairs window to throw articles of clothing and coins to the crowd below. By 1872, although he had been burned out twice, Little Jake boasted annual sales of over $200,000 during an era when a topnotch suit with two pairs of pants sold for $12 to $15.

In 1870, Seligman expanded into the rip-roaring lumber town of Saginaw. He first set up in an old grist mill on Genesee Avenue where he conducted auctions of surplus stock he had bought at bankrupty sales. Little Jake's colorful reputation preceded him, and despite a cabal of local merchants intent on running him out of town, Saginaw customers flocked to his new enterprise.

By 1874 he had dissolved his Pontiac firm and moved entirely to Saginaw. His advertising grew even more spectacular. Whether it was an Indian dressed in a scarlet British uniform carrying Little Jake's sign or an elephant accompanied by a brass band, Seligman made sure his name was not forgotten.

The gimmick Seligman is most remembered for is his disbursement of free goods. One day he road around the city in a four-horse bandwagon preceded by two brass bands while he threw clothing to the mob that trailed behind. According to an article in the *Saginaw Courier* he distributed 6,000 collars, 144 straw hats, 500 pairs of socks and 36 pairs of "good pantaloons." Two men got in a fist fight over a pair of the pants and both landed in jail.

A persistent legend, although apparently unsubstantiated in contemporary accounts, features Seligman tossing vests to a crowd of lumberjacks and offering a free matching suit to whoever retrieved them. In the ensuing melee the vests were torn to shreds. As the story goes, Little Jake kept his word about the free suit but charged the victors $12, the full price of the suit, for the replacement vest.

As Little Jake's reputation grew, his name took on an advertisng value in its own right. A local cigar maker rolled Little Jakes. A Saginaw baseball team dubbed itself the "Little Jake Club." Lumberman W.S. Gerrish bestowed the name, Little Jake, on his steam yacht. There was even a local race horse named Little Jake. Historian John Cumming of Mount Pleasant, who wrote the definitive biography of Seligman in 1978, cited the story about a local father who quizzed his young son about the state capitals. When asked about the capital of Arkansas, the boy answered, "Little Jake" instead of Little Rock.

As Seligman grew wealthier, he diversified into other investments. He bought and sold real estate and speculated heavily in shingles, lumber and pine lands. Following his purchase of a 20,300 acre tract of Upper Peninsula pine lands, the *Detroit Free Press* reported him as saying, "There is no truth in the rumor that the Upper Peninsula will hereafter be known as Seligmanville."

"Little Jake's Discount and Deposit Bank" first operated from the rear of his store but later moved to its own building on Genesee Avenue. His bank was particularly popular with the hordes of lumberjacks who descended on Saginaw each spring. They trusted Little Jake to watch over their stake while they blew the remainder on a wild binge. Seligman later became active in banks in Owosso, Lansing and Detroit. Another oft-repeated story pictures him carrying around crisp $100 bills which he signed as president of the bank before spending.

In 1890, Little Jake purchased the triangular-shaped Music Block at the intersection of Genesee, Jefferson and Lapeer and erected an imposing tower at its front. At a cost of $3,000 he installed a huge clock and the giant copper statue he claimed was himself. Most contemporaries caught the humor of the large-scale model of the diminutive merchant.

During the 1890s, Little Jake moved from Saginaw to Detroit and later to Salida, Colorado, where he died in 1911. His statue became a local landmark which continued to bring him fame long after his death. But Little Jake's statue blew down during a storm in 1940 and ended up in a scrap metal drive during World War II.

"Strike Four, You're Out!"

"Big Dan" Brouthers, star of the 1887 world champion Detroit baseball team.

Big Dan" Brouthers, who batted .419, played first base. "Hardy" Richardson at second and shortstop Jack Rowe both batted .363. Third baseman "Deacon" Jim White lagged behind the other members of baseball's "Big Four" at .341. Detroit had bought all four players for $8,500 from Buffalo in 1886 when that city dropped out of the National League. The following year, the Big Four would lead Detroit to its first and only National League pennant.

Four other Detroit players batted over .340 that season, including right fielder Big Sam Thompson at .406. Actually, none of those Detroit sluggers were quite as good as their batting averages indicated. During the 1887 season, scoring rules had been changed to allow four strikes instead of three, and walks counted as base hits. This experimental "batters' paradise" lasted one year only.

Detroit Major W.G. Thompson, a devoted baseball enthusiast, had brought major league baseball to Detroit in 1881 when he took over the National League franchise vacated by Cincinnati. The Detroit club's original mailing address was the "major's office." Not until 1896, when manager George Stallings outfitted the team in black and yellowish-brown striped stockings, would newspaper man Philip J. Reid dub them the Tigers. That name stuck, but until then they were simply the Detroits.

Major Thompson's Detroits played home games at Recreation Park near the present intersection of Brady and Brush streets. They came in fourth during their first season behind the Chicago White Stockings, the Providence, Rhode Island Grays and Buffalo. The Detroits finished 6th, 7th, 8th and 6th respectively, over the next four seasons. But thanks to the acquisition of the Big Four, they battled to second place behind Chicago in 1886.

William H. "Wattie" Watkins, a colorful player from Port Huron whose hair had turned white overnight when he got beaned by a Bay City pitcher in 1884, joined the Detroits as manager in 1886. The following year, Watkins' team fought a close season to win the National League pennant 4½ games in front of the Phillies. Detroit, with a population of approximately 150,000, went wild after defeating teams from much larger cities, including Boston, New York and Chicago.

Frederick K. Stearns, proprietor of a thriving Detroit drug company and new owner of the Detroits, wanted his team to become world champions. He challenged St. Louis Browns president Chris Van Der Ahe, who had won the American Association pennant for the third successive season, to a world series.

Since there were not set rules for such an event in 1887, Stearns' proposition seems rather unusual by modern world series standards. The teams would play 15 games, not more than one in each city except for those cities that supported both National League and American Association teams, and 75 percent of the gate receipts would go to the team that won a majority of the games. Each player of the winning team would receive the munificent sum of $100. Stearns also made a radical suggestion that two umpires be used, one stationed behind the batter and one near second base. Traditionally one lone umpire made all calls in major league games. Needless to say, it was not uncommon for such highjinks as first basemen holding runners by the back of the belt while the umpire was busy elsewhere.

Van Der Ahe agreed to the series, and that fall's traveling baseball circus was off and running. The Browns easily won the first game on their home field 6-1, and their German-American owner gloated, "No von can beat my vonder boys." The Detroit pitchers, Charley Getzein and "Lady" Baldwin, a southpaw from Hastings, buckled down. The teams journeyed to Detroit,

Pittsburgh, Brooklyn, New York, Philadelphia and Boston. By the time they arrived in the District of Columbia on October 21, Detroit needed only one more game to clinch the series. St. Louis won the morning game of the double header 11-3, and then the teams traveled by train to Baltimore for the afternoon match. Lady Baldwin pitched a 13-3 victory, and the Detroits were world champions.

Even though the series had been decided, the teams opted to play the four remaining games. The jubilant Detroits and dejected Browns climbed aboard a "Special" headed for Detroit. The whole city turned out to welcome their victorious nine. Unfortunately the Special arrived an hour ahead of schedule. Owner Stearns locked the players in the cars until the welcome party of 60 carriages reached the station.

When the dignitaries finally arrived, Stearns unlocked his team, and the major greeted them as conquering heros. Both teams were paraded through the city to the Russell House on Woodward Ave. for a gala banquet. The opposing teams sat down together and stuffed themselves with a huge seven-course dinner of roast beef, pork chops, game dishes and plenty of pickles and relishes, following which, the players mounted horse-drawn "ommibuses", drove out to the ball park and played nine innings before a "great crowd of 4,000." Lady Baldwin's 6-3 victory was briefly interrupted in the fourth inning as hometown favorite, catcher Charley Bennett, circled the bases pushing a wheelbarrow containing 520 silver dollars, contributed by fans.

In 1888, Detroit slumped to a fifth place finish. Stearns and his new partner, Charles W. Smith, were paying some of the largest salaries in the league, and they found themselves loosing money. Detroit suddenly learned, to its bitterness, that its National League franchise had gone to Cleveland. Smith and Stearns sold their world championship roster in 1889 for a total of $45,000.

Detroit was out of the big leagues, but it raised a team for the International Association, made up largely of teams around Lake Erie. In 1894, Detroit became a charter member of the Western League, which in 1901 expanded into the American League, and there the Tigers stayed.

Simon Pokagon, Potowatomi Orator

Chief Simon Pokagon, "the most highly educated Indian of his time."

The old chief stood on the speaker's platform crowded with dignitaries. Above, hung a life-sized model of the Liberty Bell. He wore an ordinary blue dress suit and tie, but his sponsors had insisted he don a war bonnet of eagle feathers. Before him stretched a sea of upturned faces, part of a throng of 750,000 who had gathered for Chicago Day at the Columbian Exposition, October 9, 1893.

Simon Pokagon, hereditary chief of a band of Michigan Potawatomi, pulled the rope that rang the "new Liberty Bell." When the last echoes of its peal had died away, Pokagon removed his headdress and began to speak. He delivered a scholarly oration on the past relations of the Indians and whites and the hope of peaceful coexistence for the future.

When he finished his address and the cheering died down, an earsplitting, rattling yell startled the crowd. It was the old Indian call signifying "approaching in peace". Chicago pioneer Fernando Jones made his way to the rostrum to greet the friend he had not seen in over 50 years. In the 1830s, Pokagon and Jones had played as children on the very site of the Columbian Exposition grounds, Jackson Park, seven miles south of the Chicago Loop.

Chief Leopold Pokagon, Simon's famous father, had signed the treaty of 1833 that ceded to the U.S. government the land on which Chicago stands. Despite this, the aboriginal inhabitants of the region came close to receiving no recognition at the Exposition.

The Columbian Exposition, a world's fair to honor the 400th anniversary of Columbus's discovery of America, was planned in such an epic manner that it was not completed until 1893, a year late. Foreign Nations and the various states of the union erected lavish exhibits to showcase their specialties. But when Simon Pokagon visited the fair shortly after its opening, he found nothing to commemorate his people.

He returned to his home near Hartford and wrote "The Indian's Greeting", a lament on the red man's demise. He printed the pamphlet on birch bark and sold it at the fair. When Chicago Mayor Carter Harrison read the work, he invited Pokagon to give an address during the special celebration on Chicago day.

Born in 1830 at a sugar camp near the present site of the village of Pokagon in Cass County, Pokagon grew up in an old Indian village near Bertrand on the St. Joseph River in southern Berrien County. He could speak no English until he was twelve, when, eager for an education, he attended Notre Dame for four or five years, one year at Oberlin College and two years at Twinsburg, Ohio. Trained for the priesthood, he learned four languages, and gained the reputation as "the best educated full-blooded Indian of his time."

Pokagon spent his summer vacations hunting and fishing with his mother and fur trader, Joseph Bertrand, in the land of the Ottawa in Van Buren and Allegan counties. On one such trip to the wilderness, he met Lonidaw Sinagaw. They fell in love and married. Lonidaw bore four children but, tragically, died in 1871 at the age of 35. Pokagon raised the small children himself.

Julia Pokagon Quingo remembered her grandfather as a very kind and cheerful man. Deeply religious, he devoted his life to assisting the priests and interpreting and mediating for his people. He loved children and wherever he went, a crowd of youngsters tagged along. Others remember Pokagon talking to the birds and animals in Potawatomi or poring over books in strange tongues. Washington Engle, a young attorney from Hartford, got lost in the woods and found his way to Pokagon's cabin. When he knocked on the door he was surprised by a tall Indian holding open a Greek testament. They became good friends. Engle provided free legal services to Pokagon's band and later published his autobiographical romance, *Queen of the Woods.*

The legal services required by Pokagon related to his campaigns to secure payment for his people, as stipulated in the treaty signed by his father in 1833 that ceded more than one million acres of land to the government. He gained an interview with President Grant in the 1870s to no avail. Repeated petitions were tied up in Congressional committees. Finally in 1894, after he had received national publicity for his work at the Columbian Exposition, a U.S. Court of Claims awarded Pokagon's band $104,626. Pokagon divided the sum equally among 272 families and despite his expenses in fighting for the settlement, he allotted only the same to himself as his followers - around $400.

Pokagon's pen flourished during the 1890's. He published a variety of articles on Indian lore and handiwork in *Harper's Monthly* and other prominent magazines of the period, as well as four additional birch-bark booklets. He grew in demand as a public speaker and traveled to Elkhart, Indiana, Liberty, Indiana and Holland, Michigan to deliver major orations.

In 1898, E.A. Burbank painted a portrait of Pokagon for the Field Museum in Chicago. It captured a face weakened by age but full of character and "radiant with interest, direct and noble in its gaze, gentle and friendly in its general expression." Burbank remembered the old chief as "one of the most kind and tender-hearted men I have ever known."

By then, he was suffering from ill health aggravated by poverty and a fire that destroyed his house and mementos. But he continued to work on his book, *Queen of the Woods.* As it was in press, he died of pneumonia at his home in Lee Township, Allegan County, on January 27, 1899. At his request, he was buried in an unmarked grave next to Lonidaw in the cemetery at St. Dominic Church on the south shore of Rush Lake in southern Van

Buren County. Nearby, three trees mark the graves of three of their children. Chicago citizens solicited for a monument in his honor, but it was never erected.

Michigan Men Helped Win the "Splendid Little War"

U.S. Secretary of War Russell A. Alger (left) and Governor Hazen S. Pingree (right) pose for the camera at the Michigan National Guard camp at Island Lake.

The troops called him "Pecos Bill" in honor of his service on the Western frontier. Hometown folks in Galesburg, Michigan, remembered "Bull Shafter," the champion wrestler. His fellow Michigan Grand Army of the Republic veterans recalled the dashing young infantry lieutenant who rose to the rank of brigadier general.

But now, in June 1898, at the age of 62, Major General William Rufus Shafter tipped the platform scales at over 300 pounds, too fat to even mount a horse. Nevertheless, "Big Bill" had been chosen to lead the 17,000 American soldiers who would invade Cuba.

The United States had declared war against Spain on April 25, ostensively to free Cuba from Spanish tyranny. But the martial ambitions of a generation who wanted to prove itself in battle and the prospect of territorial expansion were also underlying causes. The sinking of the battleship Maine in Havana Harbor on February 15 did much to solidify American public opinion.

The advent of hostilities found the U.S. Army in a deplorable state, ill-equipped and under strength. However, the modern American "steel navy" was in an advanced state of readiness. Commodore George Dewey's Asiatic squadron "remembered the Maine" on May 1, when it totally destroyed the Spanish squadron at Manila Bay while suffering no damage to American vessels. The Spanish fleet in the Caribbean commanded by Admiral Pascual Cervera y Topete quickly took refuge in Santiago harbor, where it was effectively bottled up by the naval forces of Admiral William Sampson and Commodore Winfield Schley.

Shafter's expeditionary force, under orders to reinforce Sampson and Schley and seize the port of Santiago, landed at Daiquiri and Siboney Bay to the east on June 22. Despite his corpulence and the fact that he was so ill much of the time that he needed to be carted around on a door, Shafter somehow accomplished his mission.

The Americans won the battle of El Caney and charged up San Juan Hill on July 1. Although Teddy Roosevelt and his "Rough Riders" took most of the credit for the latter battle, other American troops including two all-black regiments also performed heroically.

At a total cost of 1,572 casualties, Shafter's force captured the heights to the east and north of Santiago, thereby placing themselves in position to shell the city and the Spanish fleet in the harbor. On July 3, Cervera's fleet attempted to run the American blockade, but was destroyed during a four-hour engagement. The garrison of 24,000 Spanish troops at Santiago surrendered two weeks later and for all practical purposes the "splendid little war" was over.

Michigan folks were mighty proud of the way Big Bill whipped the Spaniards, as well as their state's other contributions to the war effort. Secretary of War Russell A. Alger was another Michigan man. A self-made lumber baron from Grand Rapids, Alger also achieved a brilliant military record in the Civil War. He enlisted as captain of the 2nd Michigan Cavalry in 1861, participated in 66 battles and skirmishes and won the rank of major general. Alger served as Republican governor of Michigan in 1885-87 and as a U.S. senator from 1902 until his death in 1907.

Progressive Governor Hazen S. Pingree, dubbed "Potato Pingree" because as mayor of Detroit during the Panic of 1893 he had allowed citizens to plant gardens on city land, was at first opposed to U.S. intervention in Cuba. But when war was declared he backed the cause to the hilt.

On April 23, 1898, President William McKinley called for 125,000 volunteers from the various state militias. Michigan's initial quota was four regiments of 1,000 men each. The following day, Pingree called out the entire National Guard to report to camp at Island Lake, a Livingston County resort. The 31st, 32nd, 33rd, and 34th

Michigan Volunteer Infantry Regiments were rapidly organized. Following McKinley's second call for volunteers in May, the 35th Michigan was also mustered.

Pingree camped out with his troops and military training began in earnest. Within the next two months, the Michigan regiments were reassigned to regular army camps at Chickamauga Park, Georgia, Camp Alger, near Washington D.C., Fort McPherson, Georgia and Tampa, Florida. At the southern camps, the men suffered from typhoid fever and other diseases. They were issued heavy wool uniforms unsuitable for the tropical climate and received substandard rations including canned meat which the troops dubbed "embalmed beef."

The 33rd and 34th regiments took part in Shafter's invasion of Cuba. Pingree was particularly proud that Michigan was the only state to have two regiments involved in the campaign. The Michigan soldiers participated in a diversionary attack on Aguadores during the Battle of San Juan Hill.

Private John Appleyard of Co. I 33rd Michigan Infantry wrote home to his parents in Benton Harbor: "We was under fire from 9 o'clock in the morning until 4 in the afternoon. I tell you it felt funny for a while but I sure was braver than at first. I did not kill any Spaniards that day but when we were on outpost I caught 2 and killed one while they were trying to pass my post."

Three of the men of the 33rd died in battle, but tropical disease was a much more effective enemy than Spanish soldiers. Fifty men of the 33rd and 88 of the 34th died of yellow fever and other diseases. Of the 6,667 Michigan troops mustered, about 250 died of disease.

Strange as it may seem, Michigan also furnished a naval brigade. Organized in 1897, the state naval reserves trained on the *U.S. Yantic* on Lake Erie. During the war, 270 men and 11 officers of the Naval

Militia of Michigan enlisted in the U.S. Navy. The *U.S. Yosemite*, which was totally manned by Michigan sailors, single-handedly blockaded San Juan, Puerto Rico. Her crew captured or destroyed several blockade runners.

The brief Spanish American War resulted in the U.S. acquisition of strategic territories including the Philippines, Guam, Puerto Rico and, indirectly, Hawaii.

Battle Creek Breakfast Boom

DR. PRICE'S

Triabita Food

The Wheat Flake Celery Food

Endorsed by dietitic experts, pure food manufacturers, and chemists. Used exclusively at the "Varsity" training table :: :: ::

Crisp, Dainty, Delicious, Appetizing

Served either cold or hot makes a perfect food for all classes of people of all ages

Prepared by the

Price Cereal Food Co.

Battle Creek, Mich.

Maddock

One of the cereal boom's strangest concoctions advertised its merits in 1903.

Charles W. Post bumped his handcart across the frozen ruts of downtown Battle Creek's Jefferson Street. It was December 1894, and Post's cart was piled high with paper bags containing a new coffee substitute he had invented, manufactured and rather immodestly named Postum. But as he peddled his product from store to store, few merchants responded to the 40-year-old entrepreneur's sales pitch.

Actually Post had borrowed the idea for Postum from Dr. John Harvey Kellogg during a stay at his world-famous health spa, the Battle Creek Sanitarium. Post, a lifelong sufferer from stomach complaints, had checked into the "San" in 1891. Post liked the health foods that Kellogg had invented, especially granola and caramel cereal coffee.

He opened up his own medical boarding house called LaVita Inn in 1892, wrote a book titled *I Am Well*, and in December 1894, went into production of Postum. Post invested $46.85 in a secondhand peanut roaster, a coffee grinder and some mixers, installed his machinery in an old horse barn next to the inn and roasted up a batch of Postum.

The initial disappointing sales improved when Post tried out the skills that would eventually win him title as "the grandfather of modern advertising." He put a small red dot and the slogan "It makes red blood" on Postum labels and invented new names for old ailments. Advertising readers learned they could be cured of "coffee heart", "coffee neuralgia" and "brain fag" by switching to Postum. They believed him, and Post sunk most of his early profits into more copy.

He sold $5,000 worth of Postum in 1895 and $265,000 worth the following year. In 1898 Post introduced a product he had adapted from Kellogg's granola, Grape Nuts, and total sales reached $840,000. By 1901, Post was spending $400,000 on advertising and clearing nearly $1 million a year. He launched a hectic building program to expand his plant on the eastern edge of Battle Creek and began putting his name on the local map. In 1901, he built the Post Tavern, a famous luxury hotel. In 1902, he financed the Post Theatre and platted an 80-acre housing development called the Post Additon.

Post's meteoric rise from rags to riches inspired a Battle Creek boom of epic proportions. Incipient cereal makers, intent on getting rich quick, flocked to the area. Approximately 80 different brands of breakfast cereals made a temporary debut during the first decade of the 20th century.

Imaginative proprietors tried every conceivable variation of baked, flaked, chopped, mushed and impregnated wheat, corn, rice and oats on the public's taste buds. Then as now, novel brand names seemed more important than ingredients.

Colorful packages of Grain-O, Grape Sugar Flakes, Malted Zwieback, Malt-Too, Malto-Vita, My Food, Flak-Ota, Cocoa Creme Flakes, Cereola and Egg-O-See greeted grocery shoppers. Most tasted about the way they sounded. Frumenta tasted pretty good, but its razor-sharp flakes cut consumer's mouths. On joker claimed that Michigan lumbermen created the cereal industry to make use of all the sawdust from their mills.

Norka, a cooked-oat cereal, drew its name from Akron, the inventor's home town spelled backwards. A local grocer called his breakfast cereal Per-Fo, short for perfect food. A Battle Creek druggist compounded Cero-Fruto, wheat flakes sprayed with apple jelly.

The cereal boom lured a pair of mechanical-minded brothers from Kalamazoo. The Fullers created Korn Krisp, which sounded good, but they left too much oil in the flakes, and the product grew moldy on grocery shelves. They were soon back in Kalamazoo tinkering with transmissions, a product that would eventually make their name famous.

Numerous Battle Creek cereal makers linked their products with University of Michigan athletes. Advertisers claimed that the Wolverine football team crunched Mapl-Flakes "by the barrel" in 1902. The track team preferred Malto-Flakes, "the rational food for men and women who wish to eat for strength." U of M fans read in their programs that "athletes who eat Bordeau Flakes never get stale," which is more than could be said for Bordeau's Boston Brown Flakes, a commercial flop.

Probably the strangest breakfast food served up at U of M training tables hailed from Yorkville, a hamlet on Gull Lake between Battle Creek and Kalamazoo. Dr. V.C. Price, a mysterious entrepreneur from Chicago, conceived the idea of impregnating wheat kernels with a celery-flavored solution. Triabita, Price assured consumers, made "a perfect food for all classes of people of all ages." Steaming bowls of celery-flavored cereal appealed to few, and the Triabita factory closed within a year.

Benjamin Morgan, a Battle Creek realtor, joined the cereal circus in 1902 with Golden Manna. Morgan offered a prize in each boxful, a ticket good for a ride on the firm's new three-seater automobile with a fringed top. The ride turned out to be a tour of his newly platted Morgan Park subdivision as well as a lengthy sales pitch.

Meanwhile, the man who had indirectly inspired the cereal boom, Dr. John Harvey Kellogg, was being left in the lurch. In 1894, when an elderly patient broke her false teeth on some zwieback he had prescribed, Kellogg invented a substitute calculated to reduce lawsuits. He named the world's first flaked breakfast cereal Granose. That or his parsimonious advertising budget sealed the fate of Granose.

In 1898, with the assistance of his younger brother, W.K. Kellogg, he switched from wheat to corn and invented corn flakes. The doctor considered the product a health food, but his brother thought it had commercial possibilities as a convenient breakfast food for well people.

When W.K. Kellogg favored a massive advertising budget and the addition of sugar, the brothers feuded. Finally, in 1906, W.K. got control of the Battle Creek Toasted Corn Flake Company, and henceforth the signature on the package was his.

W.K. Kellogg and C.W. Post became multimillionaires as a result of the Battle Creek cereal boom, but few other companies survived more than a few years. Ultimately, ready-to-eat breakfast cereal revolutionized America's eating habits and enabled homemakers to do better things with their time, which, as "Tony the Tiger" said, was just "grreaatt!"

Once Nearly Extinct, Whitetails Bounded Back

John James Audubon painted white-tailed deer in the 1830s.

The buck bounded across the barnyard, jumped a fence and disappeared into a clump of trees. Amazed citizens of the rural community of Climax, in eastern Kalamazoo County, searched for the wild animal. November's nimrods still make news, but on November 23, 1905, that deer itself made Kalamazoo Telegraph headlines. It was the first to be seen in the county since 1880 when pioneer woodsman William Glover had shot one west of Kalamazoo.

Whitetailed deer had originally been abundant in southern Michigan. Deer prefer a habitat found at the margins of forests, marshes and swamps, and southern Michigan's presettlement terrain consisting of park-like oak openings, open prairies and bogs proved ideal. Deer were less plentiful to the north because of the dense stands of virgin timber that allowed little underbrush to grow.

Deer formed a staple in the diet of the native Ottawa, Potawatomi and Chippewa. But Michigan's relatively small aboriginal population never seriously affected the deer supply. Nature in the form of wolves, panthers and harsh northern winters selectively harvested the weaker of the species and kept the herds strong and healthy.

Pioneers and early travelers to southern Michigan marveled at the number of whitetails they encountered. New York writer Charles Fenno Hoffman made a tour on horseback across southern Michigan in December 1833. He frequently saw deer feeding on the prairies. Near Tecumseh in Lenawee County he was struck by the number of pet fawns pioneer children had adopted. At one cabin "a tall hound was sitting erect beside one of these gentle creatures, who was licking the ears of the enemy of his race."

Three years later, when a cultured English lady, Harriet Martineau, journeyed across the state by stage, she also noticed a number of spotted fawns that had been tamed by children. Near Ypsilanti her stage stopped at a settler's cabin. The occupant boasted that he had shot 100 deer the previous year and sold them for $3 apiece.

Deer hunting for profit evidently formed an important part of the frontier Michigan economy. William Nowlin, who pioneered at the present site of Dearborn in 1834, penned a classic account of his experiences, *The Bark Covered House*, published in 1876. Nowlin related that he paid off the mortgage on the family farm by deer hunting as a full-time profession. After the first railroad line came through in 1838, he shipped carloads of venison to the eager market in Detroit.

A Mr. Hermit, who pioneered in Ottawa County's Jamestown Township in the late 1840s, recalled killing 86 deer in one winter. There were no state regulations governing the hunting of deer. Pioneers eager to convert the Michigan wilderness into farms considered deer a threat to crops. In 1859, the Michigan Legislature passed the first law governing deer hunting. The season was shortened to the last five months of the year. But hunters, resident or not, could still kill as many deer as they wanted. The 1859 regulation was too little and too late. The remaining herds were soon slaughtered below their minimal breeding level. By the 1880s, deer were virtually extinct in southern Michigan.

Meanwhile the logging industry had been lustily transforming northern Michigan and the Upper Peninsula's vast stands of white pine into stump lands - barren stretches of cutover land periodically ravished by forest fires. But as shrubs and other underbrush suitable for deer brouse sprouted up, the northern deer population increased. By the 1870s, well-to-do sport hunters had begun annual pilgrimages to the north country to reaffirm their masculinity.

Professional hunters also began greedily exploiting the northern herds. As the first railroads snaked their way into the north country, market hunters began shipping hundreds of tons of venison "saddles", as the choice hind quarters were called, to commission houses in the cities. During the summer these same hunters killed thousands of deer for their hides and left the meat to rot. At a meeting in Saginaw in 1882, concerned sportsmen produced evidence that more than 100,000 deer carcasses had been shipped by market hunters from northern Michigan depots during the fall of 1880.

In the early 1880s, the northern Michigan herds also began to decline. Succeeding state legislatures sought to save some deer for sportsmen by tightening hunting regulations. In 1891 the hunting season was drastically reduced, and Van Buren and Allegan counties were completely closed to deer hunting. The first deer hunting licenses appeared in 1895. For a 50-cent fee hunters could kill up to five deer. Market hunting was outlawed in 1901, and the bag limit was limited to two deer in 1905 and to one deer in 1915. Still, Michigan's deer population shrank yearly.

By the World War I years, deer had been exterminated from the lower rows of northern Michigan counties. But during the 1920s, the more stringent regulations and increased forest fire protection brought about a gradual increase in the herds. By the Depression Era, the northern Michigan herds had regained most of their losses.

In the 1920s, some tame deer escaped in northern Livingston County and gradually grew into a sizeable herd. Friction developed, however, between naturalists who enjoyed seeing an occasional deer and farmers who feared crop losses. For that reason, the Michigan Department of Conservation, forerunner to the DNR, campaigned against any efforts to replant deer in southern Michigan. Nevertheless, in the early 1930s, Allegan County Sheriff Guy Teed and other conservation-minded citizens conceived the idea of planting deer in the sparsely settled tract of land north of

Allegan that the Federal government was in the process of acquiring as a national forest.

Teed's group purchased about a dozen whitetails from the estate of the Getz Farm Zoo in Holland, Michigan. Penned up until acclimated to the wilds, the deer were released in what eventually became the Allegan State Forest. The herd prospered, and local farmers were mollified by permits that allowed them to shoot deer that were damaging crops.

From Allegan and a few other plantings white-tailed deer spread across southern Michgian. In 1941, a special hunting season was held in Allegan County. By 1952, Michigan hunters bagged over 100,000 deer during the last three days of the season. Currently, according to DNR statistics, over one million white-tailed deer roam Michigan, providing aesthetic thrills for naturalists and sport for the annual army of hunters.

The Hirsute Nine Played Ball With the Best of Them

Hirsute members of the House of David nine. (photo courtesy State of Michigan Archives).

Baseball great Grover Cleveland Alexander reared back and whipped a fast ball right down the middle of the plate. The catcher, "whose whiskers looked like Spanish moss protruding through his face mask," rifled the ball to second. The second baseman resembled one of the Smith Brothers of cough drop fame. He pegged the ball to the first baseman whose waist-length locks stirred in the breeze. The third baseman wore braids and the short stop a ponytail. The outfielders looked like biblical patriarchs. It was the hairiest team in history.

Despite its less-than-clean-cut appearance, the House of David nine played hardball with the best of them. The hirsute team, members of a communal sect founded in 1903 by Benjamin Purnell, hailed from Benton Harbor.

Purnell, born in 1861 in a log cabin near Maysville, Kentucky, had been raised in the bosom of the enthusiastic hill country religion that featured revivals and shouting preachers. As a teen-ager, he began spellbinding crowds with his own pulpit oratory.

At 16, Purnell married a local girl, but without bothering to secure a divorce, left her and wedded Mary Stollard, a 17-year-old from a neighboring county. The couple took to the road through the Great Lakes states pounding the bible and passing the hat wherever they could draw an audience.

During his travels, Purnell became associated with a fundamentalist cult called the Flying Rollers. The bearded sect had originated in 18th century England when Joanna Southcott proclaimed herself the first of seven angelic messengers referred to in Revelations. Throughout the 19th century, five more messengers made their appearance. The Flying Rollers now awaited only the arrival of the seventh messenger to announce the millennium.

Benjamin Purnell became convinced that he was, indeed, the true seventh messenger. By force of his charismatic personality and hypnotic preaching, he began gathering a coterie of disciples.

On St. Patrick's Day 1903, Benjamin and Mary arrived in Benton Harbor to establish the House of David and prepare for what he termed "the ingathering of Israel." The following year, Benjamin left for an around-the-world recruiting tour. Australia proved especially fertile and, early in 1905, Purnell and 85 Australian converts,beards and long hair waving in the breeze, marched to the tune of a brass band from the Benton Harbor train station to the colony site.

House of David cultists associated themselves with one of the lost tribes of Israel. They wore their locks long in imitation of Jesus. When new members joined the colony, they turned over all earthly possessions, and men and women lived in communal conditions, celibate and vegetarian.

Despite these rather stringent regulations, Purnell saw nothing wrong with making money. In 1908, the House of David opened an amusement park to entertain the growing number of curious tourists. While gawking at their hairy hosts, visitors could stroll through the zoo, ride the miniature railroad or dine in the vegetarian restaurant. Later, a beer garden, night club, hotel and huge cold storage plant brought in additional revenue.

The most popular moneymaker, the baseball team, got started around 1912. Colony boys were allowed to play after completing their daily tasks. They began beating teams from nearby communities and as their prowess grew, they whipped the best of the area's industrial leagues. Soon, they were on the road playing Chicago semi-pro teams.

The colony built its own ball park and organized a farm system: a boys team, a girls team, and a bearded men's team that played for Benton Harbor tourists. The first-string team barnstormed the country playing before large crowds eager to watch their bizarre brand of ball. A baseball version of the Harlem Globetrotters, they devised a fast-paced warm-up drill called "pepper." The players passed the ball around with such speed that spectators lost sight of it until it emerged from under a belt-length beard. The first baseman routinely caught pop flies behind his back, and another crack base runner sometimes stole second from third base.

Purnell augmented local talent by recruiting non-colony professional baseball players who let their beards grow to get the job. Grover Cleveland Alexander pitched for the team after he finished his major league career in 1930. The House of David manager offered Babe Ruth a $35,000 contract to play for the team in 1936 and even waived the beard requirement. The Babe declined.

In 1923, court proceedings against Purnell rocked Benton Harbor. It seems that cult dogma concerning celibacy applied to everyone except the seventh messenger. Stories began leaking out about "the king of harem heaven." Purnell went into hiding in 1923 and for nearly four years authorities searched for his whereabouts. In 1926, state police axed their way into colony headquarters and discovered him, sick and emaciated.

Following a sensational court trial in 1927 that produced 15,000 pages of testimony and 250 witnesses, including Purnell's first wife, the judge declared him a fraud and public nuisance and exiled him from the colony. But Purnell died before the sentence could be carried out.

A power struggle developed over colony assets, and a schism resulted in two House of Davids. Mary Purnell organized the City of David, and ex-lawyer Harry Dewhirst gained control over the original House of David.

Both colonies fielded baseball teams during the 1930s. At one time, Dewhirst sent out three traveling teams. Highlights during the depression era included pitching duels between Grover Cleveland Alexander and Satchel Paige, a pioneer attempt at night baseball and donkey baseball. The Depression proved too much for Dewhirst's teams, but Mary Purnell's traveling nine remained a popular attraction until her death in 1953.

Presently, a few "righteous remnants" of the House of David maintain a vigil awaiting the cataclysm that will signal the advent of the millennium, the last survivors of the hairiest team in history!

Henry's Tin Lizzie

A 1925 advertisement for the Model T tudor sedan.

Henry Ford sat perched on a stool, daydreaming, as he gazed out the window of his new factory on Piquette Street in Detroit. Suddenly he turned, tapped the knee of Eugene W. Lewis, a young Timken roller bearing salesman who sat next to him, and said slowly, "I am going to make a motor car that will be light and strong and clean so that women can drive it. And it will have enough power to do any kind of work called for, and will be sold so any man who can own an average horse and buggy can afford to own a car."

It was 1905 and Ford's prophetic statement would have seemed totally unrealistic to the average American. The automotive industry was in its infancy, and horseless carriages were still rich men's toys. Woman drivers made front page headlines. Total production of all motor vehicles numbered less than 25,000 units that year. The average cost of a car was over $2,100 at a time when most laborers were lucky to earn $15 for a 50- to 60-hour work week. The popularity of phrases such as "Get out and get under," and "Get a Horse," vouched for typical automotive reliability.

Henry Ford himself had heretofore led a somewhat checkered career in the field. Born on a Dearborn farm on July 30, 1863, Ford had early in life eschewed the drudgery of farm chores for invention. An encounter with a steam road engine when he was twelve spurred his interest in developing an automobile. Tradition has it that he built a steam-powered vehicle in the 1880s. By 1896, he had constructed his first gasoline-powered automobile.

The first two automobile manufacturing companies Ford founded failed, but in 1903, he borrowed $28,000 from a dozen associates to launch the Ford Motor Company. A lawsuit, however, threatened to end his new company during its first year of production, as well.

It seems that George P. Selden, a New York patent

attorney, had taken out a patent in 1879 for a self-propelled vehicle. He never actually manufactured a car but his patent apparently covered any self-propelled vehicle in which gasoline was used. Beginning in 1895, all American automobile manufacturers had to pay royalties to the Selden concerns. The Association of Licensed Automobiles Manufacturers granted manufacturing rights under Selden's patent to what they considered reputable companies.

When Ford sought to join the association in 1903, he was refused as a "fly-by-night crackpot." He went into production anyway and the ensuing lawsuit cost Ford millions of dollars in attorney fees. It was finally settled in 1911 with a verdict that the Selden patent only applied to two-cycle engines. Despite the litigation that hung over his head, Ford's company prospered.

In 1905, he drew national attention by offering a four-cylinder roadster, called the Model N, for $500. Orders flooded in from across the country for his first reliable vehicle that was within reach of the average wage earner. Unable to keep up with sales demands, Ford began applying some of the principles of mass production to his plant. He dropped most of his other models to concentrate on the Model N. Despite its low cost, by 1907 his profits had reached $1 million a year.

The following year, Ford announced a new model, a car that would truly revolutionize American society, the Model T. When the Model T first hit the market in October 1908, Ford was deluged with so many orders that by the end of the winter he announced that he could not accept anymore that year.

Like the Model N, the car affectionately nicknamed the "tin lizzie" was designed to appeal to the common man and especially rural motorists. It was light, weighing around 1,000 pounds, simple enough in design for home maintenance, fairly powerful and built high enough to navigate the notoriously rough country roads.

Best of all it was cheap. The original price was $825, and contrary to modern trends each year brought a reduction. By the mid 1920s, a Model T touring car without accessories sold for $260.

It was a car for the people, and they responded in overwhelming numbers. The Model T soon became the most popular automobile in the world. But despite Ford's goal to produce a car suitable for women, the Model T was a no-frills version that required both strength and mechanical ability to operate. The strength came in the starting. Motorists needed to learn to carefully adjust the spark and throttle levers on the steering column, advance to the front of the vehicle, grasp the crank and jerk it vigorously. If the engine started, they raced back to reset the controls. More than one novice suffered a broken arm or thumb when the engine backfired while cranking.

Two pedals on the floor, one for forward and one for reverse, and a side lever that also functioned as an emergency brake operated the semi-automatic planetary transmission. If the brakes were not working properly, a touch of the reverse pedal would also slow the Model T down.

Model Ts came with a set of tools, a screwdriver, monkey wrench, etc., and most drivers soon learned their purpose. There were also thirty oil holes and grease caps that required filling as often as every 100 miles of operation.

Experienced drivers also threw a ball of baling wire into the tool chest. One comedian started a rumor that they were going to magnetize the rear axle of the Ford so it would pick up the parts that dropped off.

Joke writers compiled entire books of Model T humor, such as "A Ford will go anywhere except in Society," and "Q: What shock absorbers do you use in your Ford? A: The passengers."

The dashboard of the Model T was barren of

instruments. The gas gauge was on the tank under the seat. There was no speedometer on stock models. When asked if he wanted to buy a speedometer, one owner quipped, "I don't use one. When my Ford is running five miles an hour, the fender rattles, 12 miles an hour my teeth rattle, and 15 miles an hour the transmission drops out."

Despite the jokes, the Model T democratized automobile ownership and transformed rural American life by making possible trips to town in less than a day.

Ford built a modern plant for exclusive production of Model Ts at Highland Park in 1910. By 1913, implementation of a moving assembly line had revolutionized manufacturing techniques. The following year, Ford announced the $5, eight-hour workday and tens of thousands of applicants queued up at the plant.

By 1927 when Ford suspended production to retool for the Model A, over 15 million Model Ts had rolled off the assembly line.

The Duke of Duck Island

Governor Chase Osborn at his desk in Lansing.

Sugar Island, where Chippewa once boiled cauldrons of sap to make innumerable mococks of maple sugar, lies in the St. Marys River southeast of Sault Ste. Marie. If you were to take the Sugar Island Ferry, then drive about 10 miles over dirt roads that set your teeth to chattering, you might find your way to the entrance of a nature camp owned by the University of Michigan. Follow a narrow footpath that twists through the beech forest, cross a half-submerged pedestrian bridge to Duck Island and plow through briars and sumac to a clearing on the shore of Lake George. Across the water, on the Canadian side, fancy new cottages dot the banks, but here there are only ruins.

This was the summer home and retreat of one of Michigan's most colorful personalities - Governor Chase Osborn. The log cabin, once his pride and joy, now with a leaky roof and rotting floor, is unsafe to enter. Nearby, a monolithic concrete structure with an iron door housed his library. Half-hidden in the underbrush stands a small outbuilding resembling a chicken coop. Open the door and peer in. A bed of ancient pine boughs occupies most of the floor. The hinged walls of the structure can be raised to let the cool night breezes flow. Here, Chase Osborn slept and meditated, and although he's been dead almost 40 years, you can still feel his presence.

Born in 1860 in Huntington County, Indiana, Osborn was named Chase after noted Ohio abolitionist Salmon Chase. Following a brief attendance at Purdue University, Osborn secured a position on the staff of the *Chicago Tribune*. When he was laid off in 1879, Osborn moved to Wisconsin to work at a series of Milwaukee newspapers. Two years after his marriage in 1881, Chase and Lillian Osborn settled in the rough frontier town of Florence near Michigan's Upper Peninsula boundary. Osborn ran the local newspaper, had his first taste of politics, began prospecting for iron and developed a lifelong affection for the north country.

In 1887, he sold his holdings for $10,000, a small fortune in those days, and relocated to a community he had fallen in love with during an exploratory tour of the U.P., historic Sault Ste. Marie. Osborn purchased a partnership in the *Sault News*, and built it into a thriving weekly. Income from this newspaper venture allowed him time and resources for his favorite pastimes - travel, iron prospecting and politics.

Osborn earned his first political appointment in 1890, the Sault postmastership. But when Democrat Grover Cleveland won the presidency in 1892, Osborn was ousted via the spoils system. That year, Governor John T. Rich appointed him state game and fish warden. A genuine sportsman, Osborn energetically enforced game laws but also tempered prosecution with understanding. For example, he let off with a reprimand violators who desperately needed game for food. Osborn also used his influence as game warden as an avenue for higher office.

Osborn made an unsuccessful bid for Congress in 1896, but in 1898 reform Governor Hazen Pingree appointed him state railroad commissioner. Osborn took his new post seriously. During his four years in office, he personally inspected Michigan's 11,000 miles of track, sometimes while riding in a special cab mounted over a locomotive's cowcatcher. A progressive reformer, he advocated more effective control of railroads through a regulatory commission and insisted on separated grade crossings where tracks intersected.

Following an unsuccessful campaign for the Republican nomination for governor in 1900, Osborn temporarily lost interest in politics. He sold the *Sault News* in 1901, but within a year had reentered the newspaper business as a part owner of the *Saginaw Courier Herald.* He spent months tramping the wilderness of the Upper Peninsula and Canada, hunting and prospecting. In 1900, he discovered a vast iron range in Ontario called "Moose Mountain." That and profitable timberland investments brought him a modest fortune.

In 1907, Osborn made an extended tour of South America, and in 1909 he published a two-volume narrative about his experiences, *The Andean Land.* Later works on such varied subjects as the Hiawatha myths, philosophy, Madagascar, a new theory of earthquakes and survey miscalculations ultimately swelled his bibliography to over 20 items. His autobiography, *The Iron Hunter,* published in 1918, became a best seller.

Osborn returned to the political arena in 1908, by serving as chairman of the Michigan Republican nominating delegation. He was also appointed a regent of the U of M. The following year Osborn announced his candidacy for the 1910 Republican gubernatorial nomination. Frank Knox, editor and close friend from the Sault who would later win fame as Secretary of the Navy during WW II, ran Osborn's campaign. Osborn led the campaign with his usual vigor. He conducted the first full-scale automobile speaking tour of the state, traveling 12,000 miles over Michigan's horrible roads, to deliver some 1,000 speeches, as Knox remembered, "wherever one found a crossroads, a blacksmith shop and a bird's nest."

Osborn's strong personality and zeal paid off. He won the primary by a substantial plurality. Michigan nearly always had gone solidly Republican since the party had been founded in Jackson in 1854, and Osborn's 1910 battle against Democratic nominee Lawton T. Hemans proved no exception. During his term, Osborn championed progressive causes including woman's suffrage, teaching of agriculture in public schools, bank controls, child and women's labor laws and workman's compensation. He also cut the state's bureaucracy and carefully managed expenditures to turn Michigan's debt into a ½ million dollar surplus. After two years of intense reform activity, Osborn chose not to run for reelection.

Following a world tour, Osborn campaigned for governor again in 1914 but lost to incumbent Woodbridge Ferris due to a split conservative Republican vote. He never ran for governor again but unsuccessfully sought election to the U.S. Senate in 1918 and 1930.

Despite his political losses, Osborn remained in the national spotlight as one of Michigan's most colorful promoters. He campaigned hard to secure national park status for Isle Royale and as early as 1935 advocated a bridge at the Straits of Mackinac. When the United Nations came into being following World War II, Osborn sought to seat the headquarters on Sugar Island. Called an "impractical scheme," had it succeeded the Mackinac Bridge undoubtedly would have been constructed a decade earlier.

The man known as the Sage of the Sault, The Iron Hunter, The Duke of Duck Island and Michigan's Grand Old Man died in 1949 at the age of 89 and was buried near his beloved Duck Island home.

Someone Shouted "Fire!"

Trammers descending the Tamarack Mine near Calumet, ca. 1910.

The big bushy pine tree, rugged like the copper country where it grew, had been tamed by popcorn garlands, blown glass ornaments and bits of tinsel. Beneath the Christmas tree lay a heap of little presents, one for each of the miners' children who had gathered at the Italian Hall above a saloon in Red Jacket, now part of Calumet. It was Christmas Eve 1913, and despite the bitter strike that had idled the copper miners for five long months, the woman's auxiliary of the Western Federation of Miners had wanted to do a little something for the children.

As the final chorus of "Hark! The Herald Angels Sing" died down, Kris Kringle appeared to hand out big homemade cookies and boxes of hard candy. Suddenly someone shouted "Fire!" Parents grabbed their youngsters and stumbled in panic over the rows of folding chairs for the only exit. The first to reach the steep stairs toppled down against the door at the bottom that opened in. The rest followed until the stairwell was packed tight with screaming struggling humanity. It was all over in a matter of minutes. There was no fire - only a silent pile of 74 victims. Eighteen adults, 19 little boys and 37 little girls had been smothered to death in the stairwell.

The senseless tragedy at Calumet underscored a long season of hatred and violence brought on by the copper miners' strike. Yet prior to 1913, Michigan's copper country had remained remarkably free of the labor violence that had troubled other mining districts.

In the early 1840s, hordes of entrepreneurs eager to make a fortune in red metal raced to the Keweenaw Peninsula in a frenzy that rivaled the later California gold rush. Throughout most of the 19th century, Michigan's copper country was the nation's chief source of that essential metal. The Calumet and Hecla mine, the leading producer, held the record through the 1920s as "the most profitable metal mine on earth."

Eastern owners of the Calumet and Hecla and other copper mines operated their holdings like feudal seigniories. The company owned miners' houses or the lots they stood on. It built schoolhouses and a free library, provided the land for churches and subsidized a huge bathhouse and hospital. The company offered family garden plots, free garbage removal, reduced electricity rates, and a pension and insurance fund. Practically everything was controlled by the company, including local politics and the workers' private lives.

For nearly 70 years this benevolent paternalism operated smoothly. Attempts at unionization were quickly quashed. But in 1909, the militant Western Federation of Miners secured a toe hold in the copper country. Some workers had become disgruntled over the all-pervasive paternalism. More specifically, the introduction of the one-man drill threatened the existing system.

The worst job in the mines was that of the trammer, who pushed heavy ore cars to the hoist. Unskilled immigrant laborers began as trammers and, if lucky, moved up to the relatively easier job of miner. The one-man drill, which replaced the heavier two-man drill, reduced the mining work force as well as the likelihood of advancement. What's more, working deep in the mine shaft without a partner's companionship and assistance in case of an accident was more dangerous.

By the spring of 1913, the situation had become tense. The owners refused to recognize or negotiate with the Western Federation of Miners and rumors of a strike were everywhere. The strike began on July 23. Practically every copper mine in the district closed down and 14,528 miners and 1,500 stamp mill and smelter workers were idled.

Rioting broke out at the shaft houses when some men tried to cross the picket line. The mine owners cabled

Governor Woodbridge Ferris, who promptly dispatched all available state militia units, including two artillery batteries and three brass bands. Two weeks before, the mine-owner dominated Houghton County Board of Supervisors had negotiated with the Waddell-Mahon Corporation of New York, which specialized in recruiting strikebreakers. Soon after the strike started, trainloads of hoodlums and German emigrants straight off the boats began arriving in the copper country, ostensibly to guard the mines.

Violence flared up and both sides committed atrocities. Four guards chased a miner off company property to his boarding house. When he refused to come out, they fired through the windows, killing two men. Three weeks later, someone riddled three Canadian strikebreakers with bullets as they slept. In another incident, a guard and miner killed each other during a shootout in the streets of Hurontown.

Mine owners adamantly refused to negotiate with union representatives. Attempts at conciliation by Governor Ferris proved futile. When James MacNaughton, general manager of the Calumet and Hecla properties, was asked if he would submit to arbitration by President Woodrow Wilson, he replied, "This is my pocketbook. I won't arbitrate with you as to whose pocketbook this is. This is mine..."

The Christmas Eve tragedy focused national attention on the copper strike. On Christmas Day, a Citizen's Alliance that had previously backed the mine owners raised $25,000 for relief of the stricken families. Charles Moyer, fiesty president of the Western Federation of Miners, turned down the offer with the reply, "Labor will bury its own dead." Moyer also accused the alliance of sending representatives to yell "fire" at the party.

On December 26, a vigilante committee of alliance members burst into Moyer's hotel room and demanded a retraction. When he refused, he was beat, shot in the back, dragged 1½ miles to the depot, flung on a train and warned if he ever returned to Calumet he would be publicly hanged.

Nevertheless a special congressional investigating committee reported "...the miners as a whole are not oppressively treated... there is little one can do to end the strike..." The miners voted to end the strike on April 14, 1914, and returned to work without winning recognition of their union.

The Ship Began to List, as Hundreds Hurried on Board

The Eastland docked in South Haven.

Thousands of gaily dressed excursionists streamed onto the loading pier adjacent to the Chicago River. It was Saturday July 24, 1915. The Western Electric Company, manufacturer of telephone equipment, had planned a gala picnic in Michigan City, Indiana, for its 7,500 employees.

The crew began herding passengers aboard the first steamer to be loaded, the *Eastland.* Suddenly, the ship began to list away from the dock, straining at its moorings as the gangplank lifted three feet into the air.

The ship slowly righted itself and hundreds more passengers hurried on board. Twenty-five hundred people, predominantly women and young children, had crammed aboard the vessel. The ship's band struck up a popular tune, and at 7:40 a.m., the captain gave the signal to start the engines.

Still tied to the dock, the 269-foot-long steel-hulled vessel once more began to tilt. Passengers on the top deck heard a sound like a tray of glasses being dropped and rushed to the starboard railing. As the top-heavy *Eastland* slowly continued to roll, the thick mooring ropes tore the piling from the pier.

The *Eastland* floated out into the channel of the Chicago River. Passengers scrambled to climb the tilting deck. Some jumped into the water, and minutes later, as the hull continued to topple, hundreds were "hurled off like so many ants being brushed from a table."

The *Eastland* lay on its side in 21 feet of water. Thousands of friends and relatives watched in horror the bobbing mass of humanity struggling to stay afloat in the swift current.

Wailing "babies floated like corks." Men and women clawed at anything afloat and in panic dragged each other down. Others desperately tore off their clothing so they could swim against the current. The screams of those drowning in the river mingled with the muffled cries and sounds of others trapped below the decks as the water rose inside.

Some lucky few clung to the top of the hull. One man dangled high in the air, his coat caught on a nail. He alone of his party survived.

Another woman, a good swimmer, managed to clasp her young son and daughter in either arm as she tread water. But she lost grip of her daughter and never saw her alive again.

Rescuers jumped into the murky current. One hero from New York City saved four people. Workmen began cutting holes in the steel hull and pulling out those fortunate enough to have found air pockets. After several trips below, a city diver engaged in retrieving bodies went violently insane.

It was all over within a few minutes. It took the *Eastland* about six minutes to roll on its side. Volunteers quickly made a long stretcher brigade to convey the bodies. The final death toll of 835 made this the worst naval disaster in the history of the Great Lakes.

The ill-fated *Eastland* had been constructed by the Jenks Shipbuilding Company in 1903. Her string of bad luck began at her launching in Port Huron, when she failed to meet specifications during the trial run. Naval architect W.J. Wood suggested structural modifications. The top deck was to be removed and the water ballast compartments kept filled at all times. Wood thought there was something basically wrong with the hull design and later called the *Eastland* "the crank of the lakes."

Following modifications, the Michigan Steamboat Company began using the *Eastland* in the South Haven to Chicago excursion trade in competition with another steamer, the *City of South Haven.* In 1908 a group of Cleveland investors bought the *Eastland.* "The Speed Queen of the Lakes" shifted to Lake Erie, where she made daily round trips from Cleveland to Cedar Point.

She was fast, trim and handsome. Strains of the steam calliope mounted on her hurricane deck carried for miles across the waves. The *Eastland* transported over 200,000 passengers in 1913 alone. Strange rumors persisted, however, that she was unsafe for passenger travel.

The Eastland Navigation Company offered a $5,000 reward to anyone who could prove her not seaworthy. Yet, near disasters kept happening. During her first Cleveland season, she ran aground at Cedar Point with 2,000 passengers aboard and listed heavily. In 1913, she ran ashore in the mud near Cleveland.

In 1914, the *Eastland* was back on Lake Michigan. The Graham and Morton Steamship Company had moved their dock from St. Joseph to Benton Harbor, and a rival firm bought the *Eastland* for the St. Joseph to Chicago run. St. Joseph historian L. Reber remembered the *Eastland* as a "hoodoo from the start." She broke down several times at the height of the season.

On July 24, 1915, the hoodoo became reality. Headlines around the world spread the news of yet another naval catastrophe to rival the recent *Titanic* and *Lusitania* losses. The captain and crew of the *Eastland* were put under arrest, as city, state and federal authorities began investigations.

No official cause was ever revealed. A combination of factors, including the design of the boat's hull, the overcrowding and the fact that crew members had failed to fill all the water ballast tanks, probably lay at fault. After two decades of litigation, the U.S. Circuit Court of Appeals finally found the owners not liable for the 835 deaths caused by the tragedy.

Salvage crews soon patched up the holes in the *Eastland's* hull, and righted and floated her. The U.S. government purchased the vessel in 1916 and converted her into a naval training vessel. Renamed the U.S.S.

Wilmette , she proved satisfactory in every detail well into World War II.

Aladdin: They Built Castles Overnight

A typical Aladdin home, the "Cadillac," sold for $1,392 in 1919.

Come to Washington," was all the telegram from the War Department to the Aladdin Company of Bay City stated. The following afternoon, a representative of the firm that manufactured pre-cut homes arrived at the U.S. Quartermaster's office.

"Here are the blueprints covering construction of cantonment for 800 soldiers at Fort Snelling, Minnesota. Must be completed in thirty days. Are you ready?"

"Certainly," was the reply. "Good afternoon," and the Aladdin man tucked the blueprints under his arm and rushed to the depot just in time to catch a 5 o'clock train for Bay City.

It was May 1917, and the U.S. had just entered the world war. When Wilson signed the declaration of war against Germany on April 6, the entire U.S. Army consisted of only 200,000 men. During the war, the army swelled to four million. The Quartermaster Corps rushed to build 32 new training camps with facilities for 1,800,000 men.

The Aladdin Company had easily won a building contest held by the army at Fort Meyers, Virginia, in April. It had constructed better barracks cheaper and faster than four competitors. Now Aladdin would see what it could do about building an entire fort.

When the Aladdin construction superintendent arrived at the historic little post situated near St. Paul, the commandant could tell him little about the War Department's plans, only roughly where the buildings were to be located. But a temporary Aladdin lumber mill was already on freight cars headed for the fort. Within days, the whine of high-powered saws could be heard eating their way through mountains of lumber. Arc lamps were installed so construction could proceed at night.

Gangs of carpenters beat a machine gun crescendo as waves of buildings swept over the open fields. Barracks, officers' quarters, mess halls, hot water heating plants, a water works, electric lighting and plumbing and sewer systems took shape. In 26 working days, the post stood complete and ready for troops. Aladdin had set a new record by completing one building every 63 minutes.

The Aladdin Company was the brainchild of William Joseph Sovereign, who founded it with his brother Otto Egbert Sovereign in 1906. Actually, Sovereign had gotten the idea from two Bay City companies that manufactured knocked-down boats for customers to assemble themselves. The Sovereigns decided to apply the pre-cut concept to houses and garages.

Without formal architectural training, W.J. Sovereign designed the first plans for a garage on his mother's breadboard in the family kitchen. The brothers pooled their entire savings, $20,000, and invested in a few hundred circulars and a small advertisement in *Power Boating Magazine.* They plowed their initial profits back into more extensive advertising. A Manhattan dentist bought the first "Aladdin home" in July 1907, a five-room cottage that sold for $289.

Success followed quickly for the firm which drew its name from the Arabian Nights tale about the genie who constructed a complete castle overnight. By 1915, sales topped $1 million. Two years later, annual sales numbered 3,200 Aladdin homes. In addition to military contracts, Aladdin built entire company towns. In 1914, Aladdin shipped 50 rail cars of pre-cut homes to build the entire town of Hopewell, Virginia for the DuPont Company. By 1917, the company published a special industrial housing catalog offering stores, churches, warehouses, hotels, dwellings and street layouts for complete towns of up to 3,000 population. Three years later, Aladdin had established offices and mills in Wilmington, North Carolina, Hattiesburg, Mississippi and Portland, Oregon, which, with the home office and mills in Bay City, supplied the entire nation.

Some consumers confused Aladdin's ready-cut

dwellings with shoddy prefab construction. But the company owed its success to the quality of its workmanship as well as by appealing to people with only minimal building skills who could construct their own home cheaply. Aladdin was able to pass on considerable savings to customers by buying timber wholesale and cutting it to exact dimensions, thereby eliminating the middleman and much waste. Aladdin catalogs delighted in showing how the company was able by careful cutting to utilize only 16 feet of siding where carpenters required 20 feet.

The Sovereign brothers emphasized the quality of their red cedar siding by offering to pay $1 for every knot customers found. Lavish color catalogs depicting fashionable architectural models were distributed nationwide following World War I. Consumers might select a three-room bungalow for as low as $753, an attractive three-bedroom dwelling called "The Carolina" for $2,778, or a top-of-the-line five-bedroom colonial revival, "The Villa," for $7,976.

Upon payment of 25 percent down, the company shipped everything necessary to complete the dwelling except the foundation. Detailed plans, structural lumber cut to exact length, siding, lath and plaster, paint, roofing, hardware, doors and windows and even the right amount of nails arrived at railroad sidings across the country. All the anxious homemaker had to do was get the load to the site, talk relatives and friends into a work party, spend plenty of time figuring out the plans and put up his house. Aladdin even furnished plans for a gala home-warming party complete with menus and games.

Aladdin catalogs from the 1920s also offered "extras," such as fashionable golden-oak, built-in furniture, fireplace mantles with bookshelves and two-story sun porches. Motorists could order a variety of garages to suit their respective vehicles. The 8 x 14 foot "Buick" garage, which sold for $148, was for some reason designed "just large enough to admit a Ford touring car with the top either up or down." The $623 "Packard" garage accommodated two 20-foot-long vehicles.

Bay City, according to the Sovereigns' catalogs, was "Aladdin Town." Practically all of the more than 75 styles illustrated had been erected there. The company encouraged prospective buyers to come to Bay City and inspect the "whole streets of Aladdin houses."

Aladdin sales continued brisk through the roaring '20s, reaching an all-time peak of 3,650 houses in 1926. Sales slumped during the Depression and continued slow through World War II. The early 1950s again saw annual sales exceeding 1,000 houses per year.

In 1982, the company that had sold more than 50,000 homes in 49 states and several foreign nations finally closed its doors. But in Bay City and in hundreds of working class neighborhoods across the country, durable and attractive homes survive as the Aladdin heritage.

The Polar Bears in Russia

Soldiers from the "Polar Bear" regiment in Russia.

The Communist forces attacked at dawn. The village of Nijni Gora lay deep within northern Russia some 200 miles south of Archangel. Russian artillery shells burst uncomfortably close to the log cabin where a contingent of Co. A, 339 Infantry Regiment had holed up for the night. The Americans jumped to their feet, fully dressed, but even their heavy wool trench coats offered little resistance to the numbing -45 degree temperature. The artillery barrage continued for an hour, and then the Russians, camouflaged in white, charged. Firing machine guns and rifles, with fixed bayonets, they struggled through deep snowdrifts as the Americans raked their ranks with lead.

A training exercise? An imaginary battle of World War III? On the contrary, this engagement, during which Michigan soldiers of the "Polar Bear Regiment" battled the Red Army on Russian soil, took place on January 19, 1919. Although World War I had officially ended in November 1918, for reasons unknown to the Michigan doughboys, they were still fighting and dying in desperate battles far from home. So far, in fact that most Americans never even knew they were there.

Soviet Russia, on the other hand, never forgot that American troops fought in the Russian Civil War assisting the "White Russian" army in an attempt to topple their government in its infancy. In the "American Expedition Fighting the Bolsheviki" can be traced the roots of Soviet distrust and antipathy toward the United States.

Following the Russian Revolution of November 1917, Lenin and Trotsky had eliminated Germany's eastern front by signing a separate peace treaty. That freed numerous German divisions to join in a massive spring offensive on the western front. The German offensive that began in March 21, 1918, proved so fierce that Allied leaders felt their only hope lay in getting Russia back in the war.

President Woodrow Wilson was initially opposed to American intervention in Russia to reconstitute the eastern front. But by July 1918, under heavy British and French pressure, he authorized a limited American force. Its objective was to guard military stores that would ultimately be needed by Russia when it reentered the war against Germany. Two expeditionary forces were dispatched to join other allied units in Russia. The 27th Infantry Regiment was sent to Vladivostok to guard the Trans-Siberia railroad. The 339th Infantry Regiment, made up primarily of Michigan men, supposedly better adapted to harsh northern winters, was ordered to Archangel. In addition, a battalion of engineers, a field hospital and an ambulance company from the 85th Division, which had trained at Camp Custer, joined the 339th.

The Michigan unit, which soon earned the nickname "Polar Bear Regiment," embarked for Europe in July 1918. Patriotic and enthusiastic, the soldiers yearned to get to France to fight the Germans. En route they first heard rumors of their actual destination, and when famed Antarctic explorer, Sir Ernest Shackleton, presented a series of lectures on Arctic survival, they knew for sure they were headed for northern Russia. One veteran recalled, "It came hard... to have missed the Big Show and be sent instead to an unknown country to fight an unknown enemy for an unknown reason." As the troopship plowed northward toward the Arctic Ocean, an influenza epidemic broke out, and 69 men died of its effects.

The American force disembarked at Archangel under command of British Major General F.C. Poole. The British, who had entirely different notions concerning the purpose of the expedition, soon altered President Wilson's intentions that American troops only guard supplies. British leaders believed that the Bolshevik regime was alien to western interests and threatened world security. They saw the chance not only to revive the eastern front but also to destroy the Communist government, by armed conflict if necessary. On August 1, the British had attacked Archangel with naval guns and seaplanes in support of an anti-Bolshevik coup d'etat. When the American troops arrived a month later, the bellicose nature of the expedition had been firmly fixed.

Archangel province is larger than Texas and its terrain consists mainly of tundra and dense pine forests interspersed with huge swamps. From their base of operations at Archangel, the American and Allied forces pushed into the Russian wilderness. The Bolos, as the Americans called the Bolshevik soldiers, retreated at first then counterattacked. The winter brought unusually severe weather. Temperatures reached -50 degrees and in December and January the days were only a few hours long. During the long winter months of suffering, it seemed to many of the Michigan troops that their country had forgotten them.

Atrocities, similar to later anti-Communist conflicts, occurred. When Sergeant Silver Parrish of Detroit was ordered to destroy a Russian village because of possible danger from snipers, he recorded in his diary, "My heart ached to have the women fall down at my feet and grab my legs and kiss my hand and beg me not to do it. But orders are orders... so I done my duty."

Co. A's engagement at the village of Nijni Gora represented the farthest American advance. During fierce hand-to-hand fighting the Bolos drove the contingent back. Only seven of the 46 Americans involved escaped unwounded.

In late February 1919, Wilson announced that U.S. troops would be withdrawn from Russia when the spring thaw permitted travel. But not until May did a new British relief army arrive to relieve them. In June, the Polar Bear Regiment departed from Archangel. The unit, originally nearly 5,000 men strong, had suffered more than 2,000 casualties.

An anonymous veteran of the Russian Campaign penned a parody of John McCrae's "In Flanders Fields" that expressed the feelings of many a Polar Bear.

"In Russia's fields no poppies grow
There are no crosses row on row
To mark the places where we lie,
No larks so gayly singing fly
As in the fields of Flanders

We are the dead. Not long ago
We fought beside you in the snow
And gave our lives, and here we lie
Though scarcely knowing reason why
Like those who died in Flanders"

In 1929, a commission traveled to Russia to recover the bodies of Michigan men who had been buried there. It returned with the remains of 86 soldiers which were interred near a large marble monument of a polar bear in White Chapel Cemetery, Troy, Michigan.

The Bridgman Raid

William Z. Foster, left wing union organizer, escaped the Bridgman raid in 1922.

Jacob Spolansky, head of the FBI's Chicago office, snapped opened the communication from Washington marked "urgent" and read: "Secret convention of the Communist party now in progress somewhere in vicinity of St. Joseph, Michigan. Proceed at once to locate same and keep under discreet surveillance."

It was August 19, 1922, and America was experiencing its first "Red Scare." Despite the weakness of the Bolshevik government in Russia, the West took seriously the First Communist International in 1919 that promoted a program of world revolution. A wave of strikes that year by which American labor sought to retain gains was widely blamed on communist provocation.

When unknown anarchists sent bombs through the mail to prominent officials, the American mood grew uglier. A citizen who had killed an alien for shouting "To hell with the United States" was quickly acquitted by an Indiana jury. Attorney General A. Mitchell Palmer, who had presidential ambitions, ordered a raid against alien communists on January 1, 1920. Some 6,000 persons, many of them innocent bystanders, were incarcerated.

The American Communist Party that had been formed in 1919 was driven underground. By 1922, the movement was divided over its course of action. One faction supported by Moscow wanted the party to become legal, while another championed the illegal underground. The Russian government dispatched a plenipotentiary envoy, Professor H. Valetski, to end the factional struggle within the American Communist Party.

Valetski arrived in July 1922 and began organizing a convention to be held the following month. The communists chose Bridgman, a small village south of St. Joseph, as the site because they had successfully held a similar convention there in 1920. A farm turned summer resort owned by Karl Wulfskeel lay about one mile west of Bridgman. There among the wooded sandhills the communists planned to hold their secret convention under the guise that they were a singing society on a week-long outing.

The party took elaborate security precautions. Guards were posted on nearby hills and others monitored the village. The delegates could not leave the grounds, talk to strangers, or mail letters. Little did the communists know that an FBI secret agent known as K-97 had already infiltrated their ranks.

K-97, actually Francis A. Morrow, a New Jersey shipfitter, had begun spying on radical organizations for the Department of Justice in 1919. He joined the Communist party the following year and worked his way up within the hierarchy. He gained prestige with the FBI when he supplied information that allowed them to crack the communists' secret code. Morrow succeeded in getting himself named as a delegate to the underground convention.

The convention was planned with such secrecy that none of the delegates were informed in advance where it was to be held. Comrade Morrow was told to attend a district convention in Philadelphia on August 13, 1922. There he was directed to travel to Cleveland. Three days later, he arrived in Grand Rapids via Detroit and was given a train ticket to St. Joseph. He managed to get off a letter to the FBI at Grand Rapids, but thereafter was cut off from outside communication.

FBI Director William J. Burns dispatched an urgent message to Agent Spolansky, who caught the next train for St. Joseph. Spolansky and another special agent arrived in St. Joseph on August 19, two days after the convention had begun. The local sheriff thought Bridgman a likely spot for a secret meeting. The Bridgman postmaster told Spolansky that "a bunch of foreign-looking people" had drifted into town a few days before.

The two agents wandered around the woods most of the night in a rainstorm looking for the site. The next morning, disguised in overalls, they resumed their search. They sauntered up to the Wulfskeel farm just as the delegates were finishing breakfast. Spolansky casually asked for a drink of water and chatted about renting a cottage. Meanwhile, he scanned the communists who were standing around in discussion groups. Spolansky spotted a familiar face, that of William Z. Foster, a well-known leftwing union organizer who had joined the Communist party following a trip to Russia in 1921.

Unknown to Spolansky, however, Foster had also "made" him. One of the delegates tailed the FBI agents as they made their way back through the woods to Bridgman to plan their raid. After a vigorous debate, the communists decided to flee. Couriers dispatched to Bridgman and St. Joseph rented automobiles for the getaway. Highest priority was given to the Russian envoys, those threatened with jail sentences, and aliens. A group of American citizens was charged with hiding the convention's records.

When Spolansky, three other FBI agents, the local sheriff and a posse of 20 townspeople swooped in at dawn, they were disappointed to find most of the 80 delegates had disappeared. The 17 remaining communists, including K-97, surrendered without resistance and were locked up in the St. Joseph jail. K-97 drew a map showing the whereabouts of the convention records. Agents returned to the farm and dug up two sugar barrels filled with documents, including lists of the delegates, instructions from Moscow and speech texts.

Entire books were published based on the incriminating documents which revealed what was termed "the most colossal conspiracy against the U.S. in its history." The Bridgman raid focused national attention on the tiny community. Spolansky continued to track down the delegates who had escaped his clutches. He nabbed a group of 16, including Foster, at a meeting in Chicago.

Foster's trial in April 1923 featured K-97 as a star witness. Despite the evidence, the defense, based on the right of freedom of speech, resulted in a hung jury. That same month, the Communist Party held a convention in New York City and voted to dissolve its underground organization in favor of the legal Workers' Party. In 1928, the name of the organization reverted to the Communist Party. In 1932, Foster ran for president on the Communist ticket.

Fiery ACLU attorney Patrick H. O'Brien, who was elected Michigan Attorney General in 1932, finally dismissed the cases against the other Bridgman defendants in 1933.

He Brought "God's Country" Into the Parlor

James Montgomery Flagg's sketch of James Oliver Curwood appeared on dust jackets of his popular novels.

“ ’Bring him back, alive or dead,” were Superintendent McVane’s last words.”

“And now, thinking of that parting injunction, Carrigan grinned, even as the sweat of death dampened his face in the heat of the afternoon sun.”

The staccato clicking of the old manual typewriter stopped. James Oliver Curwood leaned back from his desk. His writing studio, located in the turret of a miniature medieval castle he had built of fieldstone near downtown Owosso, commanded a sweeping view of the Shiawassee River. Curwood gazed out at the sparkling stream, but his mind was over a thousand miles away in the Canadian Northwest.

Curwood’s Mountie hero, Carrigan, had tracked the outlaw across the wilderness. But now the desperado had pinned him down with rifle fire and he was a deadly shot. How would the Mountie get out of this tight spot?

Suddenly Curwood slammed his typewriter carriage to the right and the type crackled across the page.

“His head was bare - simply because a bullet had taken his hat away. His blond hair was filled with sand. His face was sweating. But his blue eyes were alight with a grim sort of humor, though he knew that unless the other fellow’s ammunition ran out he was going to die.”

Curwood labored 12 hours that day on his novel and 12 hours the next day and the next. That was his style. The book was published in 1923 as *The Flaming Forest.* It became a best seller and furnished the plot for a 1926 Metro-Goldwyn-Mayer silent movie.

Curwood had published his first novel, *The Courage of Captain Plum,* a tale of King Strang’s Beaver Island empire, in 1908. *The Wolf Hunters, The Danger Trail, The Honor of the Big Snow,* and *Philip Steele of the Royal Mounted* followed in quick succession. By 1926, he had authored 25 fast-paced novels set predominantly in the north country, a non-fictional classic, *The Great Lakes,* and over 100 screen plays. From 1910 until well into the 1930s, one or more Curwood novels made every list of best sellers. Aficionados of red-blooded adventure tales in which heroines are beautiful and chaste and every hero has a dimple in his chin and wins in the end still comb used book shops for the likes of *Baree, Son of Kazan*, *The Courage of Marge O'Doone* and *Nomads of the North*.

The author who would supply generations of armchair explorers with wilderness adventures was born in Owosso on June 12, 1878. Curwood spent much of his childhood in Vermilion, Ohio. He owned his first gun at the age of eight and by the time he was 12 had gained a reputation as the "best hunter in Erie County." He returned to Owosso in 1891. When he got expelled from high school he took a bicycle tour of the south, hawked patent medicines for awhile, and ran a trap line along the Shiawassee. The profits he made from furs allowed him to attend the University of Michigan for two years beginning in 1898. Curwood took a job as a reporter for the *Detroit News-Tribune* in 1900 and rose to the rank of editor. He resigned in 1907 to pursue literary work entirely.

Following publication of his first novel, Curwood was employed by the Canadian government as a writer. He lived among the Indians and Eskimos, made long forays into the wilderness on snowshoes, by canoe and by pack train and developed a lifelong love for the rugged northland he would later popularize as "God's Country." Each year he returned to the Hudson Bay region or the Canadian Rockies for big game hunting.

During his heyday as a trophy hunter he once slaughtered three grizzly bears in a single afternoon. But an encounter with a gigantic wounded grizzly on a narrow mountain ledge changed his attitude toward nature. The bear spared Curwood's life and in turn he abandoned hunting for sport. He developed a religious reverence for wildlife and natural living.

In 1921, he described his naturalistic philosophy in *God's Country: The Trail to Happiness.* During the 1920s, Curwood served as chairman of the Game, Fish and Wildlife Committee of the Michigan Conservation Department (now the DNR). He campaigned for the preservation of wild species and natural habitat for the enjoyment of sportsmen as well as those "men, women and children who want to go into those same woods and fields to look and listen and feel."

When not tramping through the Canadian wilds, Curwood alternately lived at his Owosso castle and at a beautiful log lodge he built on a forest tract near Roscommon. He lived alone at his Roscommon cabin for weeks on end, without telephone, electricity or running water, dividing his time between his writing and the woods.

Cosmoplitan editor and long-time friend Ray Long once described Curwood as "a vastly peculiar man... a personality that invited misunderstanding." He had courageously faced the charge of a wounded grizzly but was morbidly afraid of snakes. He ran at the sight of a garter snake and woke guests in the night with screaming nightmares about serpents. He also apparently harbored a hair fetish. He lingeringly described his heroines' long voluptuous locks, and many female admirers sent him snippets of their hair which he preserved among his papers.

Curwood was also passionately fond of ice cream. When the C.A. Connor Ice Cream Company of Owosso, which made a product exactly to his taste, was threatened with bankruptcy, Curwood and a friend bought the creamery and kept it in operation. Curwood also liked fairs. When county officials decided to cancel the local fair because it lost money, Curwood bought the fairgrounds and continued the fairs.

Curwood was at the height of his popularity and

prosperity in 1927. He led a good clean life and told friends he expected to live to be 100. But that summer, he sent a recent portrait of himself to the editor of the *Bookman* with a prophetic message. "I might die, in which event it is possible you would be kind enough to use it." Weeks later, Curwood contracted blood poisoning. He died on August 14, 1927.

Brush Monkeys

Members of the 634th Company CCC building a log cabin at Houghton.

The Atwater Kent radio set squealed and crackled as the patriarch of the household delicately tuned the several knobs in search of just the right frequency. The A and the B batteries had been freshly charged, the long antenna connected to the steel windmill retightened and the rural family gathered to hear the broadcast. It was 7:30 p.m. Friday, April 17, 1936, and President Franklin D. Roosevelt was about to deliver another of the fireside chats that had buoyed up the nation's spirit during the worst days of the Great Depression.

Then through the big gooseneck speaker came the familiar voice of the president: "Idle through no fault of your own, you were enrolled from city and rural homes and offered an opportunity to engage in healthful outdoor work on forest, park and soil conservation projects of definite practical value to all the people of the nation. The promptness with which you seized the opportunity to engage in honest work, the willingness with which you have performed your daily tasks and the fine spirit you have shown in winning the respect of the communities in which your camps have been located, merits the admiration of the entire country."

Michigan had particular cause to take pride in the Civilian Conservation Corps. Thousands of young men, housed in wilderness camps throughout northern Michigan and the U.P., had performed heroic conservation work and their accomplishments provide a recreational legacy to today's and future generations.

The CCC, dubbed "Roosevelt's Tree Army," was one of his pet "alphabet programs." In 1932, while governor of New York, he had introduced a pilot project using 10,000 unemployed men in reforestation work. During his presidential campaign, he proposed to employ a million men in forestry work throughout the nation, and on March 31, 1933, Roosevelt signed the CCC bill into law. Three months later, 250,000 young men had been enrolled in over 1,300 camps, "the fastest large-scale mobilization of men in U.S. history."

Administered by U.S. Army officers and operated in a quasi-military fashion, CCC camps not only offered jobs for the nation's unemployed youths, but also provided many with their first taste of disciplined living.

Ten percent of the corps comprised older, unemployed military veterans, but the remainder were single males 17 to 23 years of age. Applicants were required to be U.S. citizens, unemployed, not in school and healthy. Candidates applied at local selection boards and if chosen enlisted for six-month tours. They were issued military-type uniforms and other equipment. They earned $30 per month of which they agreed to send $22 home.

Camp Custer and Fort Brady were Michigan's two CCC headquarters. Work camps sprang up across the U.P. and northern Michigan. Although corpsmen did not perform military drills, much of camp life was reminiscent of army barracks. The first camps, consisting of large tents, were later replaced by simple wooden structures.

Reveille, which came at 6:00 a.m., was followed by a round of group calisthenics and breakfast in the mess hall. The men policed the grounds and fell in for roll call and inspection. The eight-hour work day began at 7:45 a.m. The noon meal was served in the field. Following dinner at 5:30, the youths were free to attend classes or engage in recreation. They might attend social events in nearby communities providing they were in their bunks by lights out at 10 p.m. Punishment for being AWOL or other infractions ranged from K.P. duty to a dishonorable discharge.

Following a brief orientation at Camp Custer on May 2, 1933, 200 corpsmen from Detroit and Hamtramck journeyed to the Hiawatha National Forest west of Sault Ste. Marie to establish Camp Raco, Michigan's first CCC company. By the summer of 1935, nearly 17,000 corpsmen lived in 103 Michigan camps. Under expert supervision they performed a wide variety of conservation-related projects.

Known affectionately by their commanding officers as "brush monkeys," much of their daily work related to reforestation. By October 1938, over 72,000 acres had been planted with seedlings. Nearly 130,000 man-hours had been spent fighting forest fires during that same period.

The brush monkeys also constructed hundreds of wilderness bridges, cabins, latrines, and fire lookout towers and cabins. They graded more than 4,000 miles of roads, constructed 28 airplane landing fields and stocked over 100 million fish. Major projects included bridges over the Muskegon and Manistee rivers, a huge log bathhouse at Ludington State Park and a limestone picnic shelter at Indian Lake State Park.

Michigan's wildlife population and habitat also benefited from the CCC. Corpsmen relocated moose from Isle Royale to the Cusino State Game Refuge where studies were performed. At Cusino and other areas, deer-feeding projects were implemented. The members of Camp Germfask constructed a system of dams, dikes and pools, planted hundreds of acres of plants suitable for wild birds and thereby converted 95,000 acres of the Seney Wildlife Refuge into a migratory wildlife preserve.

On August 13, 1935, an advance party of pioneer corpsmen waded ashore at Isle Royale, felled trees to form a gangplank and pitched their tents at what would become Camp Siskuwit. Eleven days later the main body arrived, bringing the company strength to 191 enrollees and four officers. They spent the remainder of the year constructing campsites, fighting forest fires and other forestry work, and a hardy band of volunteers even wintered on the isolated island.

One CCC veteran described the romantic appeal of service in the Upper Peninsula: "The pioneer spirit is just realistic enough to bring out the ruggedness in us. Already we have a wilderness fever that is like a drug. The whole thing grows on you and it is hard to break away. If you can think of a lumberjack's life in the North Woods as romantic and adventurous, you can picture the life of the CCC above the Straits."

During his 1936 presidential campaign, Roosevelt sought to diminish federal expenditures by a reduction in the CCC. But the program had such wide appeal that Congress approved additional funding. A poll in July 1936 disclosed that 82 percent of Americans favored continuing the CCC. In 1939, Congress extended the program through July 1943. But the manpower needs of World War II and the consequent end of the Depression killed the CCC in 1942. The military-type training received by the millions of corpsmen stood them in good stead during their war service.

The Battle of Bulls' Run

The 1937 Flint sit-down strike drew large crowds (photo courtesy State of Michigan Archives).

The Flint police phalanx pushed toward the picket line. Pickets overturned their jalopies to form barricades. Tear gas shells thudded against the pavement as a cloud of acrid fumes enveloped the struggle. Atop the roof of Chevrolet Plant No. 2, strikers stretched inner tubes between steel girders and slung volleys of pound-and-a-half automobile door hinges on the attackers. From the midst of the melee, UAW union organizer Victor Reuther blared words of encouragement from speakers mounted on an old Chevrolet.

It was the afternoon of January 11, 1937, and the temperature stood at 16 degrees. Strikers on the roof turned plant fire hoses on the police and their uniforms froze stiff. Suddenly the wind shifted and blew tear gas fumes back in the officers' faces. The police retreated, rallied and made another rush, but were repulsed by a torrent of freezing water, hinges, pop bottles and lumps of coal. They fired into the picket line, wounding 13 strikers.

A striker's wife grabbed the microphone from Reuther and hysterically cried: "Cowards! Cowards! Shooting unarmed and defenseless men! Women of Flint! This is your fight. Join the picket line and defend your jobs, your husbands' jobs, and your childrens' homes!"

Thousands of spectators gathered to watch the battle. The police set up a line several hundred yards away from the factory and fired tear gas missiles at the pickets and through the plant windows. The shelling continued until after midnight when the police ran out of ammunition. Thus ended the encounter that became famous in labor circles as "The Battle of Bulls' Run."

The labor dispute began on December 30, 1936, when UAW members struck at Fisher Body Plant No. 1. When strikers learned that General Motors planned to move dies to Grand Rapids and Pontiac plants, they decided to protect their jobs by remaining within the factory, and the sit-down spread to Plant No. 2.

General Motors, the giant among Michigan car builders, was, despite the Depression, one of the most prosperous companies in America. But the corporation kept a tight lid on labor. Management made decisions on wage rates, speed-ups, firing and hiring without worker representation. Company-dominated unions and labor spies eliminated discontented workers and attempts at rival organization. GM countered the time-honored walkout with imported strikebreakers.

The UAW had come into existence in 1935. The following year it joined the CIO, formed by John L. Lewis to provide representation to unskilled workers who were being ignored by the AFofL. The tiny UAW determined to take on the giant corporation. The novel sit-down strike, first used in Michigan during the Flint strike, proved a powerful weapon.

Contemporary public opinion opposed sit-downs as an illegal invasion of private property. But strikers contended that General Motors was violating the Wagner Act, which guaranteed employees' rights to organize and strike peacefully.

On January 2, 1937, General Motors petitioned the Genesee County Circuit Court for an injunction. Judge Edward S. Black promptly issued a sweeping injunction that not only ordered Sheriff Thomas W. Wolcott to eject the strikers but prohibited picketing as well. Wolcott deputized an additional 175 officers, but the strikers refused to budge. Judge Black's decision lost credibility, however, when it was revealed that he owned $219,000 worth of GM stock.

Public opinion swung in favor of the union, and GM temporarily ceased to press for reissuance of an injunction. The workers presented a list of eight demands on January 4, but GM President Alfred P. Sloan, Jr. adamantly refused to deal with the UAW on a national level and blamed strikers for blocking national economic recovery.

UAW membership was actually only a small percentage of GM's work force. Of the 2,700 employees in Fisher Body Plants No. 1 and 2, for example, the strikers numbered only about 500. But they had hamstrung the corporation's entire complex dependent on auto bodies, and other plants began closing.

Tension mounted as anti-union violence flared up in Flint. Local business leaders formed the "Flint Alliance for the Protection of the Home, the Job, and the Community" and began mustering support against the strike.

On January 11, GM shut off the heat and stopped allowing food into Plant No. 2. Strikers snapped the padlock on the gate, and plant police retreated inside. The awaiting 150 Flint police attacked and the "Battle of Bulls' Run" began.

With Flint on the brink of Civil War, recently elected New Deal Democratic Governor Frank Murphy arrived in Flint and mobilized the National Guard. He ordered the troops to prevent further bloodshed and not to take sides. Amidst mounting public outcries that he was pro-labor, Murphy forced negotiations.

Finally, on February 11, 1937, the two sides signed an agreement and the strike was over. The company promised not to discriminate against the strikers, and the union would evacuate the plants. GM announced a five-cent an hour wage increase. Workers marched through the streets of Flint singing, "Solidarity forever! For the Union makes us strong."

Hundreds of sit-down strikes occurred across the country during the next two years until the Supreme Court declared them illegal in 1939. By then, the UAW had established itself as the major union in the automobile industry.

Kalamazoo: the Celery City

One of Kalamazoo's youngest celery hawkers (photo courtesy Portage Public Library).

"Celery! Peanuts! Celery!" shouted the blue-eyed, blond-haired teen-ager. In one hand he held a bag of peanuts, in the other a huge bunch of celery. Not the puny imitation they grow in California nowadays, but creamy-white, crisp Kalamazoo celery - the real stuff that made the city famous.

Motorists turning the corner at Kalamazoo and Westnedge Avenues craned their necks when they saw the celery. They need not have, for practically every street corner they passed held one or more enterprising young celery vendors. It was 1936, and travelers could not get in or out of the "Celery City" without being offered the crunchy vegetable. Down at the Michigan Central Depot, salesmen hawked from the platform and boarded the cars to dispense celery, like pillows, to startled passengers.

But why the peanuts? "Well," as one of the young Dutch vendors answered when queried, "if they don't want celery maybe they want peanuts; if they stop to buy peanuts, maybe they'll buy a bunch of celery." That kind of thinking lay behind the success of many an ambitious celery salesman and grower. It was the hard-working Calvinist immigrants from Holland that put Kalamazoo on the map as the Celery City.

Local legend has it that two Scotch brothers, James and George Taylor, first introduced celery to the Kalamazoo area in 1856. Diners at the fashionable local hostelry, the Burdick House, did not know quite what to do when first served the succulent vegetable.

They soon found out, and by 1914 George Fitch quipped "If it were not for Kalamazoo, the banqueters of the land would have to go hungry until the first course were served."

Following the Taylor's pioneering attempt, not much was done with the curious vegetable. But sometime in the 1860s, Cornelius De Bruin or John De Kam, depending on whose version you want to believe, started the commercial cultivation of celery. De Bruin, so his story goes, was walking through a local vegetable garden when he noticed a freak celery plant, known as a sport by botanists, growing among the normal variety. He asked for the specimen, and from it harvested seed used to propagate the famous Kalamazoo breed. De Kam claimed De Bruin was only one of his workers.

One thing is certain - the celery business flourished. By 1871 growers began shipping celery to other markets. Soon the amount of celery shipped from Kalamazoo by rail gave it a Michigan freight rating second only to Detroit. By the turn-of-the-century, Kalamazoo Township boasted 3,500 persons employed in celery culture on 4,000 acres of land. Comstock and Portage townships supported nearly as many celery growers. Kalamazoo had become the world's leading producer of celery and proudly swapped its old title "Burr Oak City" for "Celery City."

Geologically, the Kalamazoo area proved ideal for celery culture. The terrain, shaped like a giant bowl, contained vast stretches of muck underlaid by water-impervious clay. Celery, originally native to European salt marshes, thrived in rich swampy soil. Growers needed to add only a little salt to the soil to make a perfect environment.

Real estate speculator Paulus Den Bleyker, who settled in Kalamazoo in 1851, promoted the region among his Dutch countrymen. Many had immigrated to the land of opportunity, penniless, but with an agrarian wisdom learned through centuries of reclaiming their country from the sea. They were able to buy cheaply, small tracts of swampland avoided by earlier settlers, which by dint of hard labor they transformed into choice muck farms. Deeply religious and with an ethic of hard work, the Calvinist Dutch immigrants also believed in raising large families. These ethnic traits brought success in the celery industry.

Celery culture as practiced in Kalamazoo was a highly specialized operation. Extremely labor intensive, it demanded many long hours of backbreaking labor, hence the advantage of many children. Because the plants were so tender, nearly all farming operations had to be performed by hand.

Eight weeks after seed had been sown in hotbeds, the delicate seedlings were ready for transplanting. The wet muck lands prohibited most mechanization. Plowing could only be accomplished by horses fit with special wide wooden shoes to keep them from foundering in the mud. The Dutch farmers, themselves, retained traditional wooden shoes or "klompen," ideal for swampy work.

After plowing, entire families followed closely the cycle of celery growing. The seedlings were planted close together by hand, and water for irrigation sometimes had to be carried by the pail. Small children got the unpleasant duty of picking cutworms off the plants, too tender for insecticides.

Two weeks prior to harvesting, growers patiently lugged long planks across the fields. The planks were set up over the celery, shielding it from the sun, to blanch the plant and produce a white crispy quality. At harvest time, growers pulled the celery early in the morning, wheelbarrowed it out of the fields to be washed, trimmed, crated and shipped to dining tables across the nation, "fresh as the dew from Kalamazoo."

The demise of Kalamazoo's famous industry came about through a variety of factors. Some blame deep wells sunk by the city's many paper mills that lowered the water table. Others point to a celery blight in the 1930s, probably caused by failure to rotate crops, and increased competition from other growing regions. As late as 1939 there were still over 1,000 acres under celery cultivation in the Kalamazoo vicinity, but that number shrank yearly. By the late 1950s, as Kalamazoo adopted its new nickname, "The Mall City," locally grown celery had become a fondly remembered thing of the past.

Arsenal of Democracy

Browning .30 caliber machine guns built by the Saginaw Gear Division of General Motors helped win the war.

A sneak attack on Pearl Harbor interrupted a quiet December Sunday in 1941 and America was in the war. The world had been in a mess for years and most Americans realized that it was only a matter of time before they too, would fight; but few ever forgot where they were or what they were doing when they heard the news.

The sleeping giant had been awakened, and as a generation of young men lined up in their BVDs for military physicals, their female counterparts queued up for jobs before the gates of defense plants. Soon, "Rosie the Riveter" vied with "I've Got a Gal in Kalamazoo" in jukeboxes across the nation.

Thanks in part to General Motors President William S. Knudsen, whom President Roosevelt had appointed Commissioner of Industrial Production in 1940, the mighty Michigan automobile industry had already begun gearing up for military production. When Knudsen first accepted his job, however, Army brass had already decided that Detroit would not participate in the war.

The Army had ruled that all war industries were to be located in the interior of the country, safe from border attack. Kansas seemed safer than Detroit on the Canadian border. But Knudsen argued that the war could not be won without Detroit's established factories, knowhow and experienced personnel, and he put the Motor City back on the strategic map.

Knudsen's next battle was with the lords of the aircraft industry. When he tried to adapt auto plant mass production techniques to aviation needs, they howled that he was letting "blacksmiths attempt to make Swiss watches." He settled that debate by calling officials together for a demonstration. Mechanics broke down a Pratt-Whitney aircraft engine and two identical engines built by Ford and Buick, intermingled the parts and reassembled three engines. Each operated as smoothly as the original Pratt-Whitney.

Knudsen began his campaign to convert automobile industry technology into production of military materiel by identifying which companies could most easily manufacture the needed products. In concert with famed flier James Doolittle, he displayed all the various parts in an old plant on West Warren Street in Detroit. Representatives of more than 1,500 manufacturers, toolmakers and other suppliers toured the building. When representatives found items their plant could turn out, Knudsen awarded contracts.

Machines and tools not adaptable to war work were moved into storage and toolmakers designed new machinery to take their place. By January 1941, 24 Michigan corporations had received contracts for $1 million or more. On February 9, 1942, production of civilian automobiles came to a complete halt and the industry concentrated entirely on military needs. In addition to conversion of existing plants, the government constructed huge new arsenals and factories in Michigan. Chrysler operated a giant tank arsenal in Warren that turned out more than 25,000 General Grant, General Sherman and General Pershing tanks at a rate of up to 1,000 a month.

Michigan, and Detroit in particular, soon won the title "arsenal of democracy." General Motors became the largest defense contractor of World War II, receiving over $13.8 billion worth of prime war supply contracts during 1940-44. Ford ranked third in the nation behind aircraft giant Curtis-Wright.

Chrysler produced antiaircraft guns, light ammunition, pontoons, aircraft engines and other items. General Motors made more than 2,300 separate items ranging from minute ball bearings to 30-ton tanks, as well as airplanes and airplane engines. The Saginaw Steering Gear Division of General Motors became the first company in American history to mass-produce military firearms. By March 1942, it had put more than

28,000 Browning air-cooled 30 caliber machine guns in the hands of American servicemen. Beginning in 1943, the division also manufactured thousands of M-1 carbines at Saginaw and Grand Rapids.

Packard built thousands of Rolls-Royce aircraft engines and marine engines for PT boats. The Federal-Mogul Corporation created special silver-plated bearings for aircraft engines, and its marine division at Detroit and Greenville made hundreds of thousands of propellors for PT boats, amphibious jeeps, invasion landing craft and self-tracking torpedoes.

Studebaker produced aircraft engines and heavy-duty cargo trucks. Nash and Hudson built sophisticated military engines. At the Ford Rouge plant, designers developed a new kind of light military vehicle they called the Jeep. Ford and a Willys plant in Toledo built them.

Ford's most flamboyant contribution to the war effort was the giant Willow Run bomber plant. Designed by architect Albert Kahn and constructed at a cost of over $100 million, this super-plant covered 67 acres and its final assembly lines were more than a mile in length. Construction workers broke ground in a bean field owned by Henry Ford outside of Ann Arbor on March 20, 1941. On September 10, 1942, the first B-24 rolled off the assembly line. Built at a time when the war in the Pacific was going badly for America, the plant provided a much-needed boost to morale. Touted as "the damnedest colossus the industrial world had ever known,"Willow Run was planned to produce a B-24 Liberator bomber every hour. By June 1943, an average daily production force of 42,331 manufactured and assembled the one and a quarter million parts each bomber required. When production ceased on June 28, 1945, Willow Run had created 8,685 B-24s, more aircraft than any other American plant.

Practically every Michigan city claimed factories that made contributions to the war effort. The coveted Army-

Navy "E" Award pennant for production excellence waved over factories in Grand Rapids, Muskegon, Bay City and Iron Mountain. In Kalamazoo, the Kalamazoo Stove Company made armor plate and aircraft landing gear, the Kalamazoo Sled Company fashioned cargo toboggans for arctic ski troops and the Bowers Manufacturing Company made millions of cigarette lighters for GIs.

During the height of the war, Lt. General Brehon B. Somervell, commanding general of the Army's Services of Supply, declared, "When Hitler put his war on wheels, he ran it straight down our alley. When he hitched his chariot to an internal combustion engine, he opened up a new battlefront - a front we know well. It's called Detroit." By V-J day in 1945, the Michigan "arsenal of democracy" had delivered almost $50 billion worth of military equipment that helped put the Fuhrer in the ditch for good.

Two Gigantic Harps of Steel

Michigan advertisers were quick to capitalize on the majestic Mackinac Bridge.

The '51 Ford pulled onto the deck of the *Vacationland* - nicknamed the *"Vake"* - at the State Highway Ferry Dock at Mackinaw City. It was the afternoon of November 14, 1954, the day before the opening of deer hunting season. Behind the Ford, a new Chevy had camping gear strapped on top. Next came a '53 Cadillac, a '49 Willys Jeep, a humpbacked '39 Pontiac and a '47 Studebaker. The line of cars stretched nearly seven miles south on U.S. 31 and all the way to Cheboygan on U.S. 23.

The double-ended *Vake* could convey an average of 462 vehicles per hour. It took the 10,000 horsepower ferry 35 minutes to make the four-mile trip across the straits. The deer hunters at the end of the traffic snarl would wait 19 hours to cross into the U.P. and miss the opening hours of the season.

Other huge ferries such as the *Chief Wawatam* shuttled railroad boxcars across the straits. But because of four miles of open water, Michigan's Upper Peninsula had more economic and cultural links with Wisconsin than "down below."

Generations of "dreamers" had proposed diverse solutions to the problem. In 1884, Thomas T. Bates, editor of the *Grand Traverse Herald*, became so enthused with the completion of John Roebling's Brooklyn Bridge the year before that he editorialized that such a structure was needed for the straits. He was nearly laughed out of town. Four years later, while attending a board of directors meeting at Mackinac Island's Grand Hotel, Commodore Cornelius Vanderbilt commented "What this area needs is a bridge across the Straits."

Despite such far-sighted promotion, prevailing wisdom deemed it impossible to construct a bridge from Mackinaw City to St. Ignace. Even if the structure could be designed, theorists claimed the region's bedrock was not strong enough to support such a weight.

What's more, fierce winter storms would soon destroy anything erected.

During the 20th century, imaginative advocates proposed rather far-fetched alternatives. Horatio "Good Roads" Earle, Michigan's first highway commissioner, dreamed up the idea of a floating tunnel across the straits. Charles Evan Fowler proposed a long series of causeways and bridges that would begin at Cheboygan and hop from Bois Blanc Island, Round Island, Mackinac Island and then across to St. Ignace.

The State Highway Department published a report in 1928 that demonstrated the feasibility of a bridge directly across the straits at a cost of $30 million. But no further action was taken until 1934 when the Michigan Legislature created a Mackinac Straits Bridge Authority. They hoped to secure federal funding under President Roosevelt's New Deal programs. But plans submitted to the PWA in 1935 and the WPA in 1936 were rejected.

The Bridge Authority hired an engineering firm that reported construction of a bridge possible at a cost of around $24 million. The Highway Department financed a 4,200-foot causeway at St. Ignace as an initial step. The causeway was completed in 1941, but the outbreak of World War II killed the project and the Legislature abolished the Bridge Authority in 1947.

Bridge proponents persisted. They formed an Interpeninsula Communications Council and succeeded in convincing the Legislature to resurrect the Bridge Authority in 1950. Former U.S. Senator Prentiss M. Brown, a native of St. Ignace and long-time bridge advocate, headed the seven-member authority. The group delivered a favorable engineering report to the Legislature in 1951 which demonstrated that a safe suspension bridge could be built at an estimated cost of $76 million.

A legislative battle erupted. Antagonists claimed the

bridge too expensive, not justifiable for the sparsely inhabited U.P., while proponents cited the economic benefits possible through increased tourism. Eventually the proponents won, and Governor G. Mennen Williams signed an act on April 30, 1952, authorizing the authority to bond, build and operate a toll bridge. But as no state funding was allocated, the authority had to sell bonds on the open market. Trying to sell a bridge on the bond market proved tough, but after two unsuccessful attempts, the authority succeeded in selling two series of bonds in December 1953.

By the spring of 1954, the famous marine construction firm of Merritt-Chapman & Scott had assembled a fleet of 50 tugboats, deck scows, cement barges, naval derricks called "whirleys" and a floating concrete mixing plant to begin the submarine foundation stage of the project. It was the largest armada in the history of marine construction.

Over the next four years, 3,500 workers labored under hazardous conditions to complete the engineering marvel designed by Dr. David B. Steinman. Battling ice, waves and storms, they sunk caissons 210 feet below the water surface into bedrock and constructed gigantic concrete foundations, piers and anchorages. Some 750,000 tons of dolomite from Drummond Island went into the foundations.

The second phase, construction of the steel superstructure, began on July 2, 1955. By November, the main steel towers stood completed, 552 feet above the water. In July 1956, workers began spinning the cable, one strand at a time. By October 19, 1956, 12,500 separate wires had been spun into main cables 24½ inches in diameter. Approximately 41,000 miles of cable wire went into the structure.

The final gap was closed with steel in May 1957. The five-mile-long bridge, completed at a cost of nearly $100 million, opened to traffic on November 1, 1957. Five construction workers lost their lives over the course of the project.

Two gigantic harps of steel support the Mackinac Bridge, majestic, strong and beautiful, symbolic of the peninsulas linked. For over three decades, it has conveyed millions of visitors on a magic carpet ride, 199 feet above the straits, into the fabled land of Hiawatha.

"We're Holding Our Own," the Radio Crackled, Then Eternal Silence

The Edmund Fitzgerald, "pride of the American flag" (photo courtesy U.S. Coast Guard).

The storm spawned in the Oklahoma Panhandle roared northeast toward Lake Superior on November 8, 1975. Described at first by the National Weather Service as a "typical November storm", it gained in intensity as it raced across Kansas. During the evening of November 9, the weather service issued gale warnings for all of Lake Superior, which it upgraded to storm warnings the next morning. November storms, infamous for their sudden violence, have been the scourge of Great Lakes shipping. This one, among the worst of the century, would be a killer.

The *Edmund Fitzgerald* left Superior, Wisconsin during the afternoon of November 9 on the first leg of a routine voyage to Detroit, 400 miles across the lake to the Sault. The 729-foot vessel carried a cargo of 26,116 tons of taconite pellets, the marble-sized nodules of concentrated iron ore powder used in steel production. Built at a cost of $8.4 million in 1958, the *Fitzgerald* had been the largest ship on the Great Lakes until 1971. The carrier bore the title, "Pride of the American Flag."

About two hours out of port, the *Fitzgerald* caught sight of the *Arthur M. Anderson*, a 767-foot carrier also loaded with taconite. Northeast winds of 48 mph were lashing the waves to 10 to 12 feet. The two vessels steamed eastward, 10 to 20 miles apart, on similar courses. Captain Ernest McSorley of the *Fitzgerald*, a master mariner with 44 years of experience on the Great Lakes, radioed Captain Jesse B. Cooper of the *Anderson* early in the morning of November 10. The captains agreed to change course from the normal shipping lane paralleling the southern shore to the longer but more sheltered, northern route.

The storm grew heavier as the vessels cleared Michipicoten Island around 2 p.m. At 2:45, the *Anderson* changed course to avoid the Six Fathom Shoal area north of Caribou Island, where the rocky bottom of

Lake Superior was as shallow as 30 feet. A heavy snowstorm began with a steady 50 mph wind, and the *Anderson,* 16 miles behind, lost sight of the *Fitzgerald.* When the *Anderson's* crew tracked the *Fitzgerald* on radar, she appeared to pass much closer to the dangerous shoal than Captain Cooper wanted his ship to be.

McSorley radioed Cooper at 3:30 p.m. to report minor damage on deck and a list. He would slow his engines so the *Anderson* could catch up and keep an eye on him. Minutes later, an emergency broadcast from the Coast Guard directed all ships on Lake Superior to find safe anchorage.

Winds clocked at 90 mph had forced the closing of the locks at Sault Ste. Marie. Some vessels below the locks reported gusts of 96 mph. Monster waves out on the lake reached 25 to 30 feet in height. Even the Mackinac Bridge, where winds reached 85 mph, closed down.

Around 4:10 p.m., McSorley radioed the *Anderson* that both his radar units were out of commission, and he requested navigational assistance. An hour later, during a conversation with a nearby Swedish salt-water vessel, the *Avafors,* McSorley admitted that the *Fitzgerald* "was taking heavy seas over the deck in one of the worst seas he had ever been in." But shortly after 7 p.m., McSorley told the *Anderson*: "We are holding our own."

Shortly after, the snow stopped and visibility improved. But the *Edmund Fitzgerald* was nowhere in sight, nor could she be detected on the *Anderson's* radar screen. Within a matter of minutes, the huge vessel had disappeared without a trace!

Cooper reported the missing ship to the Coast Guard. That evening, the Coast Guard and a number of commercial vessels, including the *Anderson,* began an intensive search. The three-day effort recovered two badly mangled lifeboats, a quantity of cork life preservers and a few other pieces of flotsam. But not one of the 29 men aboard was ever found.

During a sonar search made November 22 to 25, the wreckage of the *Fitzgerald* was positively identified. It lay about 17 miles northwest of Whitefish Point in 530 feet of water. In May 1976, sophisticated underwater television cameras recorded additional information. A 276-foot-long section of the bow lay right side up on the bottom. Nearby and upside down was a 253-foot-long portion of the stern. The middle of the *Fitzgerald* had disintegrated.

What actually happened to the *Edmund Fitzgerald* is still open to conjecture. Imaginative theories ranging from an occult "Great Lakes Triangle" to a series of three huge waves called the "three sisters" have been advanced. After an exhaustive study that yielded thousands of pages of transcripts, the Coast Guard Marine Board of Investigation issued its report in July 1977. It concluded that the most probable cause was the gradual flooding of the cargo hold. Waves sweeping the length of the deck had flooded the holds as a result of poorly sealed hatch covers. As the storm increased and more water entered the holds, the *Fitzgerald* settled lower and lower until, unable to float, she plunged to the bottom.

The Lake Carrier's Association, representing 15 Great Lakes shipping companies, rejected the Coast Guard's explanation in September 1977. Defending the reliability of the hatch covers and seals in use, the association thought it more likely that the *Fitzgerald* had struck or grazed the Six Fathom Shoal, ripping open several ballast tanks that filled with water. With a draft of 27 feet, the *Fitzgerald* could have, in calm waters, passed over the 30-foot deep shoal, but in the storm she might have pounded the bottom in the trough of a wave. Testimony also revealed that the shoal actually extended a mile beyond its charted location.

The National Transportation Safety Board conducted an independent investigation and reached yet another conclusion in May 1978. Rather than water slowly leaking into the holds, the board felt that there had been "a sudden massive flooding of the cargo holds due to the collapse of one or more hatch covers" caused by heavy waves overrunning the deck.

The debate as to why the *Edmund Fitzgerald* plummeted to the bottom of icy Lake Superior with its crew of 29 probably will never be fully resolved. One thing, only, is certain. Despite technological marvels, mankind has yet to conquer the irresistible force of what the Chippewa worshipped as Gitche Gumee.

BIBLIOGRAPHY

1. Fort St. Joseph

Alvard, Clarence W. "The Conquest of St. Joseph, Michigan by the Spaniards in 1781," *Michigan History Magazine.* Vol. XIV, 1930. p. 398.

Cunningham, Wilbur N. *Land of Four Flags: An Early History of the St. Joseph Valley.* Grand Rapids, (1961).

Dunbar, Willis F. *Michigan: A History of the Wolverine State.* Grand Rapids, (1965).

Kinnaird, Lawrence. "The Spanish Expedition Against Fort St. Joseph in 1781, A New Interpretation," *Mississippi Valley Historical Review.* Vol. XIX, 1932. p. 173.

__________. *Spain in the Mississippi Valley.* In *Annual Report of the American Historical Association for 1945.* Vol. 2. Washington, 1949.

McCoy, Daniel. "Old Fort St. Joseph," *Michigan Pioneer and Historical Collections.* Vol. 35, 1907. p. 545.

Mason, Edward G. "The March of the Spaniards Across Illinois." In *Chapters from Illinois History.* Chicago, 1901.

Quaife, Milo M. *Chicago and the Old Northwest 1673-1835.* Chicago, (1913).

Webster, Mildred. *French St. Joseph: Le Poste de la Riviere St. Joseph 1690-1780.* Decatur, Michigan, (1986).

Wharton, Francis, ed. *The Revolutionary Diplomatic Correspondence of the United State.* Washington, 1889. Vol. V. p. 363.

2. Father Gabriel Richard

Farmer, Silas. *The History of Detroit and Michigan.* 2nd ed. 2 vols. Detroit, 1889.

Girardin J.A. "Life and Times of Rev. Gabriel Richard," *Michigan Pioneer and Historical Collections.* Vol. 1, 1874-76. p. 481.

Greenly, A.H. *A Bibliography of Father Richard's Press in Detroit.* Ann Arbor, 1955.

Osborn, Chase S. *Father Gabriel Richard.* N.P., (1936).
Woodford, Frank B. and Hyma, Albert. *Gabriel Richard, Frontier Ambassador.* Detroit, 1958.
3. Lewis Cass
Bayliss, Joseph E. and Estelle L. and Quaife, Milo. *River of Destiny: The Saint Marys.* Detroit, 1955.
Chapman, Charles H. "The Historic Johnston Family of the 'Soo'," *Michigan Pioneer and Historical Collections.* Vol. 32, 1901. p. 305.
Doty, James Duane. "Official Journal, 1820," *Wisconsin Historical Collections.* Vol. XIII, 1895, p. 163.
Dunbar, Willis F. *Lewis Cass.* Grand Rapids, (1970).
__________: *Michigan.*
Fowle, Otto. *Sault Ste. Marie and Its Great Waterway.* N.Y., 1925.
Schoolcraft, Henry. *Summary Narrative of an Exploratory Expedition to the Sources of the Mississippi.* Philadelphia, 1855.
__________. *Personal Memoirs...* Philadelphia, 1851.
Smith, Alice E. *James Duane Doty, Frontier Promoter.* Madison, (1954).
Woodford, Frank B. *Lewis Cass, The Last Jeffersonian.* New Brunswick, 1950.
4. Henry Rowe Schoolcraft
Mason, Philip P., ed. *Schoolcraft: The Literary Voyager or Muzzeniegun.* East Lansing, 1962.
__________, ed. *Schoolcraft's Expedition to Lake Itasca.* East Lansing, 1958.
Osborn, Chase S. and Stellanova. *Schoolcraft-Longfellow-Hiawatha.* Lancaster, 1942.
Schoolcraft: *Memoirs.*
__________. *The Myth of Hiawatha.* Au Train, 1984.
Williams, Mentor L., ed. *Schoolcraft's Indian Legends.* East Lansing, 1956.
5. Mackinac Island Fur Trade
Dunbar: *Michigan.*
Fuller, Iola. *The Loon Feather.* N.Y., (1940).

Johnson, Ida A. *The Michigan Fur Trade.* Lansing, 1919.
Michigan Writers Project. *Michigan: A Guide to the Wolverine State.* N.Y., (1941).
Williams, Meade C. *Early Mackinac: A Sketch Historical and Descriptive.* Au Train, 1986.
6. William Beaumont
Burr, C.B., ed. *Medical History of Michigan.* 2 vols. Minneapolis, 1930.
Cushing, Harvey, *The Life of Sir William Osler.* 2 vols. Oxford, 1925.
Garrison, Fielding H. *An Introduction to the History of Medicine.* Philadelphia, 1929.
Osler, William. "A Backwoods Physiologist," in *An Alabama Student and Other Biographical Essays.* London, 1908.
Wood, Edwin O. *Historic Mackinac.* 2 vols. N.Y., 1918.
7. First Hanging in Michigan
Burbey, Louis H. "History of Executions in Michigan," *Michigan History Magazine.* Vol. 22, 1938. p. 443.
Catlin, George B. *The Story of Detroit.* Detroit, 1926.
Colton, Calvin. *Tour of the American Lakes...* 2 vols. London, 1833.
Stark, George W. *City of Destiny, the Story of Detroit.* Detroit, 1943.
8. The Black Hawk War
Armstrong, Perry A. *The Sauks and the Black Hawk War.* Springfield, 1887.
Brown, E. Lakin. "Autobiographical Notes," *Michigan Pioneer and Historical Collections.* Vol. 30, 1900. p. 454.
Dunbar: *Michigan.*
Durant, Samuel. *History of Kalamazoo County.* Philadelphia, 1880.
History of Berrien and Van Buren Counties. Philadelphia, 1880.
Quaife: *Chicago.*

__________, ed. *Life of Black Hawk.* Chicago, 1916.
Sagendorph, Kent. *Stevens Thomas Mason, Misunderstood Patriot.* N.Y., 1947.
Stevens, Frank E. *The Black Hawk War.* Chicago, 1903.
Utley, Henry M. and Cutchen, Bryon M. *Michigan as a Province, Territory and State...* 4 vols. (N.Y.), 1906.
9. Michigan Statehood
Dunbar: *Michigan.*
Gilpin, Alec R. *The Territory of Michigan.* East Lansing, 1970.
Millis, W. "When Michigan Was Born," *Michigan History Magazine.* Vol. XVIII, 1934, p. 208.
Utley and Cutchen: *Michigan.*
10. The University of Michigan
Dunbar, Willis E. *The Michigan Record in Higher Education.* Detroit, 1963.
Farrand, Elizabeth M. *History of the University of Michigan.* Ann Arbor, 1885.
Gray, Jane Loring, ed. *Letters of Asa Gray.* 2 vols. Boston, 1893.
Peckham, Howard H. *The Making of the University of Michigan.* Ann Arbor, (1967).
Sagendorph Kent. *Michigan, the Story of the University.* N.Y., 1948.
Shaw, Wilfred. *The University of Michigan.* N.Y., 1920.
11. The Ague
Buley, R. Carlyle. *The Old Northwest, Pioneer Period, 1815-1840.* 2 vols. Bloomington, 1950.
Burr: *Medical History.*
Riley, Henry H. *The Puddleford Papers, or, Humors of the West.* N.Y., 1856.
Van Buren, Anson De Puy. "The Fever and Ague...," *Michigan Pioneer and Historical Collections.* Vol. 5, 1882. p. 300.
12. Alphadelphia
Golab, Eugene O. *The "Isms," a History and Evaluation.* N.Y., (1954).

Noyes, John Humphrey. *History of American Socialisms.* Philadelphia, 1870.
Van Buren, Anson De Puy. "The Alphadelphia Association, its History in Comstock, Kalamazoo county," *Michigan Pioneer and Historical Collections.* Vol. 5, 1882. p. 406.

13. The Underground Railroad

Barnes, Charles. "Battle Creek As a Station on the UndergroundRailroad," *Michigan Pioneer and Historical Collections.* Vol. 38, 1912. p. 279.
Dumond, Dwight. *Antislavery.* Ann Arbor, 1961.
Glover, L.H. *A Twentieth Century History of Cass County, Michigan.* Chicago, 1906.
Haviland, Laura. *A Woman's Life Work.* Cincinnati, 1881.
Olin, C.C. *A Complete Record of the John Olin Family.* Indianapolis, 1893.
Stewart, Roma Jones. "The Migration of a Free People," *Michigan History.* Vol. 71, No. 1, Jan/Feb 1987.
Thomas, Pamela. "A Station on the Underground Railroad," *Michigan History.* Vol. 37, 1953. p. 178.

14. The Man with the Branded Hand

History of Ottawa and Muskegon Counties. Chicago, 1882.
Kyes, Alice Prescott. *Romance of Muskegon.* Muskegon, 1974.
Whittier, John Greenleaf. *Complete Poetical Works.* Boston, 1880.
Wilson, James Grant and Fiske, John, eds. *Appleton's Cyclopedia of American Biography.* 6 vols. N.Y., 1888.
Wilson, Henry. *History of the Rise and Fall of the Slave Power in America.* 3 vols. Boston, 1872.

15. Holland

Hyman, Albert. *Albertus C. Van Raalte and His Dutch Settlements in the United States.* Grand Rapids, 1947.
Lucas, Henry S. *Netherlanders in America.* Ann Arbor, 1955.

Pieters, Aleida J. *A Dutch Settlement in Michigan.* Grand Rapids, 1923.
Van Hinte, Jacob. *Netherlanders in America.* Grand Rapids, (1985).
Van Koevering, Adrian. *Legends of the Dutch.* Zeeland, 1960.
16. Lansing, The State Capitol
Darling, Birt. *City in the Forest.* N.Y., 1950.
Edmonds, J.P. *Early Lansing History.* Lansing, 1944.
Goodrich, Enos. "Locating the State Capitol at Lansing," *Michigan Pioneer and Historical Collections.* Vol. 8, 1885. p. 121.
Kestenbaum, Justin L. *Out of a Wilderness.* (Woodland Hills, 1981).
Potter, Theodore Edgar. *The Autobiography of.* (Concord, 1913).
Williams, A.L. "Removal of the State Capitol from Detroit," *Michigan Pioneer and Historical Collections.* Vol. 8, 1885. p. 130.
17. Birth of the Republican Party
Deland, Charles Victor. *Deland's History of Jackson County.* Logansport, 1903.
Dunbar: *Michigan.*
Morris, Richard B., ed. *Encyclopedia of American History.* N.Y., 1953.
Proceedings at Celebration of the Fiftieth Anniversary of the Birth of the Republican Party... Detroit, 1904.
18. King Strang of Beaver Island
Collar, Helen "The Irish Migration to Beaver Island," *The Journal of Beaver Island History.* Vol. 1, 1976, p. 27.
Fitzpatrick, Doyle. *The King Strang Story.* Lansing, (1970).
Legler, Henry E. *A Moses of the Mormons.* Parkman Club Publications. Milwaukee, 1897.
Quaife, Milo. *The Kingdom of St. James.* New Haven, 1930.
Riegel, O.W. *Crown of Glory.* New Haven, 1935.

Strang, Mark A., ed. *The Diary of James J. Strang.* East Lansing, (1961).
Utley and Cutcheon: *Michigan.*
Weeks, Robert. "The Kingdom of St. James and Nineteenth Century American Utopianism," *Journal of Beaver Island History.* Vol. 1, 1976, p. 9.
19. The Sault Canal
Bald, F. Clever. *The Sault Canal Through 100 Years.* Ann Arbor, 1954.
Dunbar: *Michigan.*
Fowle: *Sault Ste. Marie.*
Harvey, S.V.E. and Voorhis, A.E.H. *Semi-centennial Reminiscences of the Sault Canal.* Cleveland, 1905.
Moore, Charles, ed. *The Saint Marys Falls Canal.* Detroit, 1907.
Quaife: *River of Destiny.*
20. Lincoln's Kalamazoo Speech
Bartlett, D.W. *The Life and Public Services of Hon. Abraham Lincoln.* N.Y., 1860.
Dunbar, Willis F. *Kalamazoo and How It Grew.* Kalamazoo, 1959.
Starr, Thomas I., ed. *Lincoln's Kalamazoo Address Against Extending Slavery.* Detroit, 1941.
21. General George Custer
Faust, Patricia L., ed. *Historical Times Illustrated Encyclopedia of the Civil War.* N.Y., (1986).
Frost, Lawrence A. *The Custer Album.* Seattle, (1964).
__________. *General Custer's Libbie.* Seattle, (1976).
Hunt, Frazier. *Custer, the Last of the Cavaliers.* N.Y., 1928.
Isham, Asa B. *An Historical Sketch of the Seventh Regiment Michigan Volunteer Cavalry.* N.Y., N.D.
Kidd, J.H. *Personal Recollections of a Cavalryman.* Ionia, 1908.
Whittaker, Frederick. *A Popular Life of Gen. George A. Custer.* N.Y., (1876).
Wilson and Fiske: *Appleton's Cyclopedia.*

22. The Capture of Jefferson Davis
Allegan Gazette. 30 November 1907.
Hanna, A.J. *Flight Into Oblivion.* Richmond, 1938.
Harrison, Burton N. "The Capture of Jefferson Davis," *The Century.* November 1883, p. 134.
History of Allegan and Barry Counties, Michigan. Philadelphia, 1880.
Lawton, G.W. "Running At the Heads: Being an Authentic Account of the Capture of Jefferson Davis," *Atlantic.* September 1865, p. 342.
Robertson, John. *Michigan In the War.* Lansing, 1882.
Stedman, Wm. P. "The Pursuit and Capture of Jefferson Davis By an Eye-Witness. "*The Century.* February 1890. p. 594.
Wilson, James Harrison. "Pursuit and Capture of Jefferson Davis By the Commander of the Union Cavalry." *The Century.* February 1890, p. 586.
23. Sinking of the Sultana
Berry, Chester D. *Loss of the Sultana and Reminiscences of Survivors.* Lansing, 1892.
Faust: *Encyclopedia of the Civil War.*
Larson, Cedric A. "Death on the Dark River," *American Heritage.* Vol. VI, No. 6, October 1955, p. 49.
24. Logging, White Pine
Beck, Earl Clifton. *Lore of the Lumber Camps.* Ann Arbor, 1948.
Hargreaves, Irene M. and Foehl, Harold M. *The Story of Logging the White Pine in the Saginaw Valley.* (Bay City, 1964).
Holbrook, Stewart H. *Holy Old Mackinaw.* N.Y., 1938.
Michigan Log Marks. East Lansing, 1941.
Reimann, Lewis C. *When Pine Was King.* (Ann Arbor, 1952).
Russell, Curran N. *The Lumbermen's Legacy.* Manistee, 1954.
Stroebel, Ralph W. *Tittabawassee River Log Marks.* Saginaw, 1967.

25. The Fire of 1871
Appleton's Annual Cyclopedia. N.Y., 1871.
Goodspeed, E.J. *History of the Great Fires...* N.Y., (1871).
Holbrook, Stewart H. *Burning an Empire.* N.Y., 1943.
Luzerne, Frank and Wells, John G. *The Lost City...* N.Y., 1872.
Michigan State Board of Agriculture. *Tenth Annual Report.* Lansing, 1871.
van Reken, Donald L. *The Holland Fire of October 8, 1871.* (Holland, 1982).
26. Petoskey's Bay View
Baker, Emma Lamb. *Stories of Bay View.* Caldwell, 1925.
Fennimore, Keith J. *The Heritage of Bay View.* Grand Rapids, (1975).
Wheeler, Clark S. *Bay View.* Petoskey, 1950.
27. Grand Rapids Furniture City
Lydens, Z.Z., ed. *The Story of Grand Rapids.* Grand Rapids, 1966.
McCracken, S.B., ed. *Michigan and the Centennial.* Detroit, 1876.
Ransom, Frank Edward. *The City Built On Wood.* (Ann Arbor, 1955).
White, Arthur. "Grand Rapids Furniture Centennial," *Michigan History Magazine.* Vol. 12, 1928, p. 267.
28. Liberty Hyde Bailey
Dorf, Philip. *Liberty Hyde Bailey, an Informal Biography.* Ithaca, (1956).
Rodgers, Andrew Denny, III. *Liberty Hyde Bailey.* Princeton, 1949.
Warner, Mrs. Frank T. "Dr. Liberty Hyde Bailey - The Boy in Michigan." *Thru the Garden Gate.* May/June 1958. p. 9.
29. The Passenger Pigeon
Hedrick, U.P. *The Land of the Crooked Tree.* N.Y., 1948.
Mershon, W.B. *The Passenger Pigeon.* N.Y., 1907.

30. Featherbone Corsets
Carney, James T., ed. *Berrien Bicentennial.* Stevensville, 1976.
Coolidge, Orville William. *A Twentieth Century History of Berrien County, Michigan.* Chicago, 1906.
Fisher, David and Little, Frank. *Compendium of History and Biography of Kalamazoo County, Michigan.* Chicago, 1906.
The Region of Three Oaks. Three Oaks, 1939.
"The Story of Featherbone," *Featherbone Magazinette.* Autumn 1901. p. 24.
31. Seney
Martin, John Bartlow. *Call It North Country.* N.Y., 1944.
Michigan Writers Project: *Michigan.*
Reimann, Lewis C. *Incredible Seney.* (Ann Arbor, 1953).
32. Little Jake of Saginaw
Cumming, John. *Little Jake of Saginaw.* Mount Pleasant, (1978).
Gross, Stuart D. *Indians, "Jacks," and Pines.* N.P., 1962.
Michigan Writers Project: *Michigan.*
Mills, James Cooke. *History of Saginaw County.* 2 vols. Saginaw, 1918.
Mitchell, William K. *Bicentennial History of Saginaw County 1776-1976.* Saginaw, 1976.
33. Detroit Tigers
Lieb, Frederick G. *The Detroit Tigers.* N.Y., (1946).
Stark: *City of Destiny.*
Turkin, Hy and Thompson, S.C. *The Official Encyclopedia of Baseball.* Jubilee ed. N.Y., (1951).
34. Simon Pokagon
Baroux, Father Louis. *An Early Indian Mission.* (Berrien Springs, 1976).
Buechner, Cecila Bain. *The Pokagons.* (Berrien Springs, 1976).

Clark, Edward B. *Birds of Lakeside and Prairie.* Chicago, (1901).
Claspy, Everett. *The Dowagiac - Sister Lakes Resort Area and More About Its Potawatomi Indians.* Dowagiac, 1970.
__________. *The Potawatomi Indians of Southwestern Michigan.* Dowagiac, 1966.
Hodge, Frederick Webb. *Handbook of American Indians.* 2 vols. Washington, 1912.
Hulst, Cornelia Steketee. *Indian Sketches.* N.Y., 1912.
Pokagon, Simon. *Queen of the Woods.* Hartford, 1899.
35. Spanish American War
Dunbar: *Michigan.*
Freidel, Frank. *The Splendid Little War.* Boston, (1958).
Galesburg Area Centennial. Galesburg, 1969.
Millis, Walter. *The Martial Spirit.* Boston, 1931.
Morris: *Encyclopedia of American History.*
Official Souvenir. Michigan Volunteers of '98. Detroit, (1898).
Utley and Cutcheon: *Michigan.*
36. Battle Creek, Cereal City
Carson, Gerald. *Cornflake Crusade.* N.Y., (1957).
Lowe, Berenice Bryant. *Tales of Battle Creek.* Battle Creek, (1976).
Massie, Larry B. and Schmitt, Peter. *Battle Creek: The Place Behind the Products.* (Woodland Hills, 1984).
Powell, Horace B. *The Original Has This Signature - W.K. Kellogg.* Englewood Cliffs, (1956).
37. Whitetail Deer
Bartlett, I.H. *Whitetails: Presenting Michigan's Deer Problem.* Lansing, 1938.
Burt, William H. *The Mammals of Michigan.* Ann Arbor, 1946.
Gregory, Tappan. *Deer At Night In the North Woods.* Springfield, 1930.
Hoffman, Charles F. *A Winter In the West.* 2 vols. N.Y., 1835.

Kalamazoo Evening Telegraph. 23 November 1905.
Martineau, Harriet. *Society In America.* 3 vols. London, 1837.
Nowlin, William. *The Bark Covered House.* Detroit, 1876.
Pahl, John. Oral Interview. 17 June 1987.
Smith, Richard P. "Michigan's Whitetails Then and Now," *Michigan Outdoors.* February 1987. p. 14.
38. House of David Baseball Team
Fogarty, Robert S. *The Righteous Remnant.* Kent, Ohio, (1981).
Kirshenbaum, Jerry. "The Hairiest Team of All," *Sports Illustrated.* Vol. 32. April 13, 1970. p. 104.
A Book of Remembrance. Benton Harbor, 1931.
39. The Model T
Beasley, Norman and Stark, George W. *Made in Detroit.* N.Y., (1957).
Lacey, Robert. *Ford, the Men and the Machine.* Boston, (1986).
Lewis, Eugene. *Motor Memories.* Detroit, 1947.
Nevins, Allan. *Ford, the Times, the Man the Company.* N.Y., 1954.
Olson, Sidney. *Young Henry Ford.* Detroit, 1963.
Page, Victor W. *The Model T Ford Car.* N.Y., 1924.
Partridge, Bellamy. *Fill 'er Up!* N.Y., (1952).
White, J.J. *Funabout Fords.* Chicago, 1915.
40. Chase S. Osborn
Beal, Vernon L. *Promise and Performance.* Ann Arbor, 1950.
Grubbs, Lillie Martin. *Chase Salmon Osborn.* N.P., (c. 1935).
Osborn, Stella Brunt. *An Accolade For Chase S. Osborn.* Sault Ste. Marie, 1940.
Osborn, Stellanova. *Eighty and On.* Sault Ste. Marie, 1941.
Osborn, Chase S. *The Iron Hunter.* N.Y., 1919.
__________, ed. *The "Soo." Scenes In and About Sault*

Ste. Marie, Michigan. (Grand Rapids, 1983).
Warner, Robert M. *Chase Salmon Osborn.* 1860-1949. Ann Arbor, 1960.
41. Copper Strike
Barkell, William and Salmi, Wilbert E. "Strike!" in *A Most Superior Land.* (Lansing, 1983).
Gates. William B. *Michigan Copper and Boston Dollars.* Cambridge, 1951.
Jensen, Vernon H. *Heritage of Conflict.* Ithaca, 1950.
Murdock, Angus. *Boom Copper.* N.Y., 1943.
Sullivan, William A. "The 1913 Revolt of the Michigan Copper Miners," *Michigan History.* Vol. 43 No. 3, 1959. p. 294.
42. Eastland Disaster
Bowen, Dana Thomas. *Lore of the Lakes.* Daytona Beach, 1940.
Images of the Past From the Collection of Richard Appleyard. South Haven, 1984.
The New York Times. 25 July 1915.
Reber, L. Benj. *History of St. Joseph.* (St. Joseph), N.D.
43. Bay City Bungalows
Aladdin Homes Catalog No. 31. N.P., 1919.
Aladdin's Magazine. Vol. X No. 3, January 1918.
Butterfield, George E. *Bay County, Past and Present.* Centennial Ed. Bay City, (1957).
Schweitzer, Robert and Davis, W.R. "Aladdin's Magic Catalog," *Michigan History.* Vol. 68 No. 1, Jan/Feb 1984. p. 25.
44. Polar Bear Division
Costello, Harry J. *Why Did We Go to Russia?* Detroit, (1920).
Doolen, Richard M. *Michigan's Polar Bears.* Ann Arbor, 1965.
Halliday, E.M. *The Ignorant Armies.* N.Y., (1960).
Hunt, George A. *The History of the Twenty-Seventh Infantry.* Honolulu, 1931.

Moore, Joel R., Mead, Harry H. and Johns, Lewis E. *The History of the American Expedition Fighting the Bolsheviki.* Detroit, (1920).
York, Dorothea. *The Romance of Company "A," 339th Infantry.* (Detroit, 1923).
45. The Bridgman Raid
Coan, Blair. *The Red Web.* Chicago, (1925).
Dilling, Elizabeth. *The Red Network.* Chicago, (1934).
Draper, Theodore. *The Roots of American Communism.* N.Y., 1957.
Link, Arthur S. *American Epoch, A History of the United States Since the 1890's.* N.Y., 1955.
Oneal, James. *American Communism.* N.Y., 1927.
Whitney, R.M. *Reds in America.* N.Y., 1924.
46. James Oliver Curwood
Curwood, James Oliver. *The Flaming Forest.* N.Y., 1923.
__________. *God's Country, the Trail to Happiness.* N.Y., 1921.
__________. "Thou Shalt Not Kill--" *American.* December 1927.
Kunitz, Stanley J. and Haycraft, Howard. *Twentieth Century Authors.* N.Y., 1942.
Long, Ray. "Jim Curwood." *Bookman.* November 1927. p. 289.
Schmitt, Peter J. *Back to Nature: The Arcadian Myth in Urban America.* N.Y., 1969.
41. CCC
District Annual 1937, Fort Brady CCC District Sixth Corps Area. (Baton Rouge, 1937).
Hoyt, Ray. *"We Can Take It," a Short Story of the C.C.C.* N.Y., (1935).
Michigan Department of Conservation. *Ninth Bienniel Report.* 1937-1938. N.P.
Rosentreter, Roger L. "Roosevelt's Tree Army," *Michigan History.* May/June 1986.
48. Flint Sit-Down Strike

Fine, Sidney. *Sit-Down: The General Motors Strike of 1936-1937.* Ann Arbor, (1969).
Howard, J. Woodford. "Frank Murphy and the Sit-Down Strikes of 1937." *Labor History.* Vol. 1, Spring 1960. p. 103.
Reuther, Victor G. *The Brothers Reuther and the Story of the U.A.W.* Boston, 1976.
49. Kalamazoo
Dunbar: *Kalamazoo.*
Massie and Schmitt: *Kalamazoo.*
50. Willow Run
Bingay, Malcolm W. *Detroit Is My Own Home Town.* Indianapolis, (1946).
Carr, Lowell J. and Stermer, James E. *Willow Run.* N.Y., (1952).
Dunbar: *Michigan.*
Lacey: *Ford.*
Massie and Schmitt: *Kalamazoo.*
Out of the Valley to Victory. Saginaw Gear Division, General Motors Corporation. (Saginaw, 1943).
Woodford, Arthur M. *Detroit and Its Banks.* Detroit, 1974.
51. Mackinac Bridge
The Mackinac Bridge Souvenir. N.P., 1958.
Ratigan, William. *Straits of Mackinac: Crossroads of the Great Lakes.* Grand Rapids, (1957).
Steinman, David B., and Neville, John T. *Miracle. Bridge at Mackinac.* Grand Rapids, (1957).
52. Edmund Fitzgerald
Hemming, Robert J. *Gales of November: The Sinking of The Edmund Fitzgerald.* Chicago, (1981).
Stonehouse, Frederick. *The Wreck of the Edmund Fitzgerald.* Au Train, 1977.

INDEX

C

D

M

Q

R

Larry B. Massie is a Michigan product and proud of it. He was born in Grand Rapids and grew up in Allegan. Following a tour in Viet Nam as a U.S. Army paratrooper, he worked as a telephone lineman, construction laborer, bartender, and in a pickle factory before earning three degrees in history from Western Michigan University.

He honed his research skills during an eight-year position with the W.M.U. Archives and Regional History Collection. He left in 1983, to launch a career as a freelance historian specializing in the heritage of the state he loves. An avid book collector, he lives with his wife and workmate Priscilla, and their 25,000-volume library, in a one-room schoolhouse nestled in the Allegan State Forest. Sons, Adam, Wallie, and Larry Jr., as well as a border collie named Maggie, and Jiggs, a huge saffron-colored feline, insure there is never a dull moment.

Author - (photo courtesy Kalamazoo Gazette, Rick Campbell, photographer).

PLEASE RETURN TO:

P.O. Box 308
Marquette MI 49855

CALL TOLL FREE
1-800-722-9925

Your complete shipping address:

____

____

____

____

Fold, Staple, Affix Stamp and Mail

____

____

____

____

Avery
COLOR STUDIOS

P.O. Box 308
Marquette MI 49855